AF706288

BUILD A PREDICTIABLE NEW-CLIENT ENGINE

VETERINARY MARKETING

HANDBOOK FOR PRACTICE GROWTH IN AN AI ERA

CEBRON WALKER

Includes The 7 Principles for Predictable, Profitable Growth

Veterinary Marketing: Handbook for Practice Growth In an AI Era

Copyright © 2026 by Cebron Walker

All rights reserved.

No part of this publication may be reproduced, distributed, or transmitted in any form or by any means, including photocopying, recording, or other electronic or mechanical methods, without the prior written permission of the publisher, except in the case of brief quotations embodied in critical reviews and certain other noncommercial uses permitted by copyright law.

For permission requests, write to the publisher at the address below, with the subject line "Attention: Permissions Request."

Published by Walker Kreative
507 S. Prospect Ave., Clearwater FL 33756
walkerkreative.com · cebronwalker.com

This book is intended to provide general information and guidance on veterinary practice marketing. It is not a substitute for professional legal, financial, or business advice specific to your practice. The author and publisher disclaim any liability arising directly or indirectly from the use of this book.

All trademarks, service marks, and trade names referenced in this book are the property of their respective owners and are used for identification and reference purposes only. No endorsement by or affiliation with any trademark holder is claimed or implied.

First paperback edition 2026

ISBN: 979-8-9972478-0-5

Cover design by Deseray Woods
Interior design and typesetting by Deseray Woods / Walker Kreative

Printed in the United States of America

Kind Words

"Our veterinary hospital has been working with Cebron and Walker Kreative for several years now. They have really supported us with marketing strategies and the renovation of our website. I get compliments all the time now from our clients as well as prospective team members and doctors about how warm, welcoming and real our website is... really showing everyone how our team cares for their patients with a unique layout with real pictures and client testimonial videos. They have been a real asset!"

— **Dr. Jamie Ronchetto, California**

"Our time with Cebron and the WK team has been great! They built us an incredible website, helped coordinate amazing and professional media, and really helped us keep a pulse on our marketing efforts. We saw significant increase in our new clients while working with them. We have recommended them to so many colleagues. Great team, great company."

— **Dr. Kim Stewart, Texas**

"Walker Kreative is one of the best investments we could have made for our clinic! Insightful, easy to work with, very knowledgeable, Cebron and his team are totally amazing!"

— **Brandie Gibbons, New York**

"Working with Walker Kreative has allowed me to focus on being a better veterinarian and practice owner while leaving the marketing to experts. Marketing takes significant time and effort, and I never felt I could give it the attention it deserved. Their team has been wonderful to work with, and I highly recommend them to any practice owner looking to grow their business."

— **Dr. Stevenson, Iowa**

"We could not be happier with Walker Kreative! Cebron and his team have done an amazing job creating video content for our business, managing our social media content, and driving our website development. The WK team is very quick to respond to our needs, and everyone is very professional. The results have been terrific!"

— Marc Kinney, Arizona

"Cebron and his team really took the time to understand our vision. They re-did our website and made it easy to make corrections. I'm confident this will help us gain more SEO."

— Doris Zimmerman, Pennsylvania

"I have enjoyed working with Cebron and his entire team. They have provided me with excellent service and are quick to respond to any questions. I would recommend them to any business owner who wants an easy transition to adding digital marketing to their marketing plan."

— Dr. Stacey Funderburk, Illinois

"Thanks to Cebron and his team for coming out to our clinic in Nevada to create videos for us. They brought Hollywood to our clinic to make us look awesome."

— Dr. K. Moriarty, Nevada

"An overall excellent experience. Great ideas and excellent production. I highly recommend Walker Kreative and their services!"

— Dr. Anne Luther, Florida

This book is dedicated to my wife who is my life, my future. Since the day I first got the guts to talk to her, everything great in my life has been a direct influence of her. She makes me want to be the best I can be at helping others.

TABLE OF CONTENTS

CHECKLISTS, CHEAT CODES & PLAYBOOKS

INTRODUCTION

I'm pleased and genuinely grateful to welcome you to *Veterinary Marketing*. When the idea for this book first formed, I kept talking myself out of writing it. Marketing trends change constantly. Tools come and go. Platforms rise and fall. And a few years ago, the term "AI" wasn't even in our vocabulary, let alone transforming the way we run our businesses.

But over the last decade of helping veterinary practice owners grow, I realized something important: while the tools of marketing change, the laws of marketing do not. The fundamentals stay the same. When you understand the underlying principles, you simply adapt new technology for easy wins and exciting growth.

As the great David Ogilvy — considered by many to be the father of advertising — once said, "Times may have changed. The mediums have definitely changed. However, what makes us tick fundamentally as humans is the same 100 years ago and will be the same 100 years from now."

For years, I've worked closely with veterinarians who were deeply committed to serving their communities with compassionate, high-quality medicine. These practices are more than businesses — they are community cornerstones. Independent, doctor-owned veterinary practices rely on their local communities for their livelihood, but they also give back in powerful, tangible ways. Every practice supports families through the staff they employ, reinvests revenue into local suppliers and restaurants, partners with shelters and rescues, and helps shape the health and well-being of the entire area it serves. When a veterinary practice thrives, the community around it does too.

And while I was able to help many of these doctors grow predictable, healthy practices, I kept thinking about the countless others I hadn't reached yet. Maybe that's you. I wish I could have put this book in your hands sooner.

Although this book is called *Veterinary Marketing*, the truth is that it's about something much bigger. When you get your marketing right, you get back something incredibly valuable: freedom. Freedom to plan. Freedom to grow. Freedom to fund new projects, hire great staff, upgrade your equipment, and create stability — not just for your practice, but for the people who depend on it.

When your marketing is really humming along, you gain the freedom to bring your bigger dreams to life — whether those dreams are for your practice, your family, or a passion you've always wanted to turn into something more. Maybe that's a sports center for your community, a comic shop, a pottery studio, or simply another way to give back using the success you've created.

The seed for this book was planted several years ago at a church barbecue, under a line of old sycamore trees — children laughing in the background — when a colleague asked me, somewhat philosophically, "What are you?" Without a pause, and somewhat to my own surprise, I said, "A dream maker." It was one of the most truthful things I've ever said, and I still believe it today.

What made that moment so significant wasn't just the answer — it was the feeling behind it. My colleague wasn't asking what I did for a living. He was acknowledging what I brought to the world. And for the first time, I truly received it. After years of doing the work, building campaigns, coaching business owners, and pouring everything I had into helping others grow — something in me recognized that I had proved my worth. Not to anyone else. To myself.

That moment felt like a green light. It was time to press down on the gas. Time to take everything I had learned across 35 years in public relations and marketing — inside Fortune 500 boardrooms and alongside community clinic owners — and use it to reach as many people as possible. Not just as a consultant, but as a coach, a mentor, and a leader who could help others unlock the very best in themselves and in their businesses. This book is part of that mission.

I'm not a professor of marketing, and I don't hold a business degree. What I do have is more than 35 years of hands-on experience — working inside Fortune 500 companies and alongside small business owners alike. I've built campaigns that influenced entire nations and campaigns that supported a single community clinic. My goal was never simply to make companies richer. My goal has always been to help people and enrich their lives.

Think of this book as a manual, a guide, and a companion. Inside, you'll find the essential online marketing activities your practice must master to grow in today's digital-first world. You'll find examples, tactics, and step-by-step techniques that build trust, increase visibility, and strengthen your brand. With that foundation, your ads, social posts, blogs, and other marketing efforts will finally work together — pulling clients toward you instead of you chasing them.

My recommendation is to read this book the way you'd use a workbook: with a pen in hand, writing in the margins, capturing ideas specific to your practice and your community. Every chapter is designed to spark insights and help you implement what you learn quickly.

As I finish writing *Veterinary Marketing*, I'm more convinced than ever that any owner can follow this system and succeed. In fact, I believe it's nearly impossible to apply these principles consistently and not transform your practice — and, by extension, your life and the community you serve.

Welcome to the start of that transformation.

PART ONE

YOUR FOUNDATION FOR GROWTH

The Core Principles That Make the Rest of Your Efforts Effective

Chapter One

WHY MOST VETERINARY MARKETING FAILS

(AND WHAT FINALLY WORKS)

> *"Our job is to connect to people, to interact with them in a way that leaves them better than we found them, more able to get where they'd like to go."*
>
> — Seth Godin, Pioneer of Modern Marketing

Most veterinary practices waste a lot of money on marketing. And you certainly didn't become a veterinarian to figure out how to advertise or decode Google algorithms.

Yet here you are—running a practice that depends on a steady flow of new clients to stay profitable, keep the doors open, pay your staff well, and achieve the lifestyle you worked so hard for.

"I don't know if anything is working. I've been running Facebook ads for two years and see nothing," Marc told me in our *first call. "It seems like we still get most of our clients from word of mouth. And on top of that, I'm so frustrated with our website!"*

When I started working with Marc and his wife, Dr. Jeannine, at their Sedona, Arizona practice, they had already tried magazines, newspapers, shopping supplements, Facebook ads, and Google ads. They were also stuck with a website company whose proprietary software made updates slow and painful. Marc told me that weeks would go by when they asked for website updates as simple as changing a staff picture of a toxic employee they had to let go.

They wanted to do good marketing. They were willing to try things. They did exactly what the ad professionals told them on sales calls. But they had no strategy. They jumped from one tactic to the next with no real plan for building reputation, awareness, trust, and then ads that feed off an already established brand in the community.

It wasn't working. Every new idea felt disjointed and disconnected. Marc was frustrated, and Dr. Jeannine simply didn't have time to think about it—she was doctoring all day and parenting two busy young boys the rest of the time.

Marc and Dr. Jeannine were not unique. Marketing for veterinary medicine is different. Your buyer is emotionally attached to the patient. The stakes are high. Trust matters more than anything. And most generic marketing advice just isn't specific enough. This Book Is.

I've been helping veterinarians all over the country for close to ten years. In the pages that follow, you'll learn a clear, proven, veterinary-specific system for generating a predictable, steady flow of new clients—without gambling your budget, burning out your team, or turning yourself into a full-time marketer who's asking ChatGPT a few too many questions. We'll remove the guesswork, replace it with tried-and-true strategy, and put you back in control.

Is This Book For You?

Let's lay the foundation. This book is for you if you are the owner or managing DVM of a small animal, equine, or mixed practice with 3–25 staff. It's also for lead associates with partnership responsibilities and practice managers who oversee marketing. And it's perfect for veterinary students who have the dream of one day owning and running your own practice.

This Book Is For You If:

- **You believe in science, clarity, ethics, and measurable results.** You're allergic to fluff and "hacks." You're responsible with money and time. You prefer systems over trends.
- **You're frustrated by inconsistent appointment flow.** You want predictable new-client flow with a marketing plan that pays for itself—and then some.
- **You need a system that respects your time and your team's bandwidth.** Not one that creates more noise and more tasks on an already full plate.

✓ ***If any of those descriptions sound familiar—taken right from conversations I've had over the years—you're in the right place!***

Why Tactics Alone Don't Work

Your practice needs a predictable, steady flow of new clients. But marketing has often felt like a gamble—and Vegas isn't your jam.

The consequences of a disjointed, unplanned marketing approach are real: stress over whether you'll cover payroll, uncertainty about your next month's schedule, and stalled plans for office expansion or new services.

Traditional approaches fail because they're built on tactics—ads, posts, radio spots, mailers—instead of systems: a repeatable process that turns strangers into booked appointments. When you run isolated tactics, you get isolated results. What you need is a connected marketing approach that builds a trusted brand and guides pet owners from discovery to booking to long-term loyalty.

WHY IT HASN'T WORKED

If your past marketing efforts fizzled, it's not because you didn't try hard enough. It's because you were working from the wrong blueprint. Here are the most common reasons veterinary marketing fails:

Generic Strategies Built For Other Industries

Restaurant and e-commerce marketing is built around impulse buying. Veterinary care is not. Pet owners weigh risk, trust, emotional comfort, and then price. Generic marketing advice skips right over that.

Channel-First Thinking

There's a rush to "run Google Ads" or start posting on TikTok because it's a trendy platform your audience might be using. These may or may not be the right moves—but the error is not basing the effort on a strategy first. The proper order is:

- **Message**
- **Market (your audience)**
- **Mechanism (the channel)**

✓ ***When the message and the audience aren't defined, even the best channels won't deliver the results you're hoping for.***

Vanity Metrics

Impressions, likes, and website traffic don't necessarily equal booked appointments. I'm not saying your practice doesn't need those things. But if they don't ultimately lead to phone calls, forms filled out, and scheduled appointments, then you—or your marketing group—are focused on the wrong numbers and missing the strategy piece described above.

A Bumpy Path To Booking

Pet owners need a clear, frictionless path to schedule. That means clear calls to action, easy-to-navigate service pages, fast text or web-chat options that have an AI integration for quick information, responsive front desk staff, and trust-building reviews. Missing any of these links will cost you clients who clicked your ad or found your website through social media and word of mouth. Setting up and testing all of these pathways—and removing friction where you find it—is essential.

Slow Follow-Up

Many clinics lose 20–40% of their opportunities because inquiries via phone or contact forms aren't returned quickly, or social DMs go unanswered. Most so-called "marketing problems" are actually conversion problems. Studies consistently show that the likelihood of converting a new inquiry into a booked appointment drops dramatically with every passing minute. A practice that responds within 5 minutes is many times more likely to book that client than one that responds an hour later.

No Tracking, No Learning

Marketing improves through iteration. Without simple tracking—source → booked → revenue—you can't build on what's working or cut what isn't. Every month becomes a random experiment.

Are you tracking each new client and finding out where they came from? A simple new-client survey, combined with Google Analytics can tell you just about everything. Your data does not need to be so overly complicated that you need an MIT-educated consultant. If you've been frustrated about not knowing which channel to invest in, this is how you fix it.

We'll solve all of this—methodically.

A VETERINARY-SPECIFIC SYSTEM

This book gives you a repeatable marketing system tailored specifically to veterinary medicine. It's designed to:

- **Attract** qualified local pet owners and farm clients
- **Convert** interest into booked appointments
- **Retain** first-time clients for long-term loyalty and higher lifetime value
- **Measure** what's working so you can invest with confidence

You don't need to become a marketer. You need a blueprint for a new-client engine—one that reflects how pet owners actually choose a veterinary provider. That blueprint begins with clarity.

Let's be explicit: <u>the primary goal is to generate a steady, predictable flow of new clients every month while keeping existing clients engaged and loyal.</u>

Everything in this book aligns to that goal. We're not chasing awareness for awareness' sake. We're not trying to "go viral." We're not asking ChatGPT what to do and handing the answer to a team member and hoping for the best. You need a system that fills your schedule, stabilizes revenue, and creates room to plan, grow, and breathe—so you can build the practice you dreamed of.

Getting a marketing system like this in place will also:

- **Increase** the lifetime value of each client through built trust and loyalty
- **Reduce** your cost per new client by improving conversion rates

- **Differentiate** your practice on trust, clarity, and convenience
- **Protect** your brand through consistent, authentic reviews
- **Smooth out** operations related to marketing

Today You've Got Better Tools

The basic laws of marketing haven't changed in thousands of years. Merchants in ancient Rome's Trajan Market painted billboard-style graffiti, sponsored gladiator games, and paid "influencers" to push their products and services. What has changed are the tools and tactics—and today's are considerably higher-tech.

Here's what the modern marketing landscape looks like for veterinary practices:

Social Media Shows The Real You. Your social profiles—whether Facebook, Instagram, or TikTok—are a living window into your clinic, your doctors, and your care philosophy. Videos and photos that appear in a client's or potential client's feed—doctors examining patients, staff handling animals, behind-the-scenes moments from the clinic or farm—quietly answer the most important question pet, horse, and livestock owners have: Can I trust you with what I love and depend on?

Reviews = Trust. Pet owners scan ratings and read a handful of recent reviews. They aren't seeking perfection; they're seeking patterns: kindness, clear communication, gentle handling, transparent pricing, and follow-through. Your reputation is now a public asset.

Search And Maps Dominate Discovery. When a cat limps, a puppy needs vaccines, or a mare is foaling, owners grab their phone and search: "vet near me," "emergency vet [city]," or "equine vet [region]." If you don't show up prominently in Google Search and Maps, you're invisible in those critical moments.

AI Now Influences Who Gets Recommended. Pet and livestock owners are increasingly turning to AI-powered tools for guidance, not just search engines. Platforms like Google Gemini, Claude, Grok, Perplexity and ChatGPT surface answers from clear, credible online information. For independent veterinary clinics, this means your expertise, services, and reputation must be easy for both people and machines to understand. AI doesn't replace Google—it shapes which practices are referenced as trusted options when owners ask for help. Much still to come about AI as a tool to support your practice as a business and your marketing.

Convenience Wins. A clear website, web chat, quick texting, and a fast-responding front desk convert fence-sitters. If booking feels like a hassle, they'll call the clinic down the street.

Competition Has Intensified. Corporate chains and urgent care models are expanding with strong brand recognition and large ad budgets. Yes, Banfield or VCA may appear first in search results because of those massive budgets—but local independent clinics can still win. You compete not by spending more, but by being more authentic, relevant, and human. This is exactly the right time to get your marketing straightened out.

Not Every Channel Matters Equally. For most general practices, local SEO + Google Ads + reviews + conversion infrastructure will outperform "doing everything everywhere." For equine or mixed practices, regional targeting + referral networks + field service scheduling carry more weight. Knowing where to focus is half the battle.

Economic Selectivity. Clients compare prices and value. Clear preventive care plans, transparent estimates, and flexible payment options reduce friction—without discounting your expertise.

This book accounts for all of it and will help you channel your energy where it counts most.

YOUR NEW MARKETING FRAMEWORK

In the chapters ahead, I'll walk you through my 7-part marketing framework built specifically for veterinary practices. Here's a preview of how it all fits together.

1. Message–Market Fit

Before any website update or ad campaign can succeed, you must be crystal clear about who your practice serves — whether that's small animal, feline-only, exotic, equine, or farm-based clients — and whether your community is suburban, urban, or rural. Everything flows from understanding that audience.

Once you know who you serve, the next step is articulating why your practice is different in ways that actually matter to those clients. That might include your handling philosophy, same-day sick visit availability, commitment to low-stress feline care, field service capabilities, or species-specific expertise.

When your message aligns with the right audience, your homepage and core service pages begin answering the three silent questions every client asks before picking up the phone:

- Can you help with my specific need?
- Can I trust you with my animal?
- How do I book right now?

✓ ***Your message must answer all three — clearly, simply, and confidently.***

2. Findability

This is the work of making sure your practice is visible exactly where pet owners are searching. That includes your local search presence, a complete and accurate Google Business Profile, and consistent name-address-phone information across the internet. It also means a well-built, humanized website with strong service pages for the conditions and procedures your ideal clients are already looking for.

When I say "humanized," I mean this: your website needs real pictures and videos of you and your practice — not stock photography. This is a key point in standing out and building trust.

Take a quick look across the internet and you'll find that a high percentage of veterinary websites use cute stock photos of dogs and cats. What you see far less often are sites featuring the actual staff of that clinic working with real animals and real clients — service pages that show real work, real services, real people. That kind of website stands apart from the competition and builds trust fast.

A strong findability foundation is also supported by a healthy, steady flow of reviews. The process for gathering them isn't complicated: ask at the right moments in the client journey and make it incredibly easy to leave a review using QR codes, SMS prompts, or short staff scripts.

3. Reputation & Social Proof

Trust is the currency of veterinary marketing. Before a new client ever walks through your door, they've already been forming an opinion about your practice — and that opinion is shaped largely by what other people say about you online. Your Google reviews, star rating, and the way you respond to feedback all send powerful signals to prospective clients.

This part of the framework is about building and protecting your reputation intentionally. That means creating consistent systems to gather reviews, responding to every review — positive or negative — with professionalism and warmth, and letting your reputation do the heavy lifting of building trust before the first phone call is ever made.

4. Social Media & Community Presence

Social media isn't about going viral or chasing followers.

For a veterinary practice, it's about showing up consistently in the community you already serve. It's about being present, being human, and being helpful — so that when someone in your area needs a veterinarian, your name is already familiar.

This part of the framework covers how to use social media strategically without it consuming your time. You'll learn what to post, how often, and how to use your content to reinforce your message, showcase your team, and stay connected to the pet owners in your community. Done right, social media becomes one of your most affordable and powerful trust-building tools.

5. Demand Capture

This phase is about capturing the interest that already exists in your market — not just creating it. Clients who are actively searching for help right now are far more ready to book, which makes Google Ads and other high-intent channels powerful tools when used properly. Well-written search campaigns, relevant ad extensions, and appointment-focused landing pages allow you to meet urgent needs at the exact moment those needs arise.

You'll also learn how to stay present for people who visit your website but don't immediately book, through gentle remarketing that keeps your practice top of mind until they're ready to take action.

6. Conversion Infrastructure

Once you've attracted interest, this phase is about removing friction and making it easy for clients to say yes. A prominent "Book Now" button, streamlined online scheduling, and text-enabled phone lines reduce confusion and encourage immediate action.

At the same time, your front desk becomes a major part of your marketing engine. Their ability to respond quickly, communicate warmly, and guide clients toward the right appointment can make or break your results.

One of the most important concepts I'll cover later in the book is "speed-to-lead" — simply put, how fast your team responds when a potential new client reaches out. Whether it's a phone call, a web inquiry, or a text message, the speed of that first response has a direct impact on whether that person books or moves on to the next clinic on their list. You'll learn how to set clear response-time standards for your team, along with inquiry and estimate templates and follow-up workflows that make sure no opportunity slips away.

7. Retention & Lifetime Value

Growth doesn't come only from new clients. It comes from keeping the right clients for life. The most effort and expense in marketing goes into getting them through the door the first time — but that's just the beginning. With a structured welcome sequence for new clients, thoughtful preventive care programs, seasonal reminders, and useful educational content through blogs and social media, your clients stay engaged, connected, and genuinely proud to call you "their" vet.

When you communicate consistently, you reduce surprise urgent-care visits, increase compliance, and deepen the bond between the client and your practice. Clients who feel known, cared for, and valued don't just stay — they refer their neighbors, their coworkers, and everyone at the dog park. That kind of relationship isn't just good medicine. It's the most powerful marketing you'll ever do.

Every new client who walks through your door for the first time represents real marketing dollars spent. The longer they stay, the more those dollars multiply — and that lifetime value is where your marketing investment truly pays off many times over.

Putting It All Together

These seven parts aren't seven separate to-do lists. They are one connected system — each part building on the last, each one making the others more effective. When your message is clear, you get found more easily. When you're found, your reputation does the convincing. When your reputation is strong, your ads convert better. When your ads convert, your front desk closes the loop. And when your front desk closes the loop, you earn clients who stay for life.

That's The System. That's What This Book Is About.

In the chapters ahead, we'll go deep on each of these seven parts — with practical strategies, real examples, and clear steps you can begin implementing right away. Whether you're just starting to build your marketing foundation or you're looking to sharpen a system that's already working, there's something in every chapter for you.

This is the operating system we'll build together. It's designed to reduce decision fatigue, stabilize your pipeline, and give you the one thing every practice owner wants most: a steady, predictable flow of great clients — growing at whatever pace fits your practice.

THREE PRACTICES, ONE SYSTEM

Let me illustrate what I'm talking about with three real-world scenarios. As you read through them, I'm sure you'll start thinking about how you can apply these same shifts in your own practice.

Scenario A: Small Animal Suburban Clinic

Dr. Alvarez runs a one-doctor small animal practice with four staff. He's "tried everything"—sporadic social media posts, boosted posts, a local billboard, a coupon in a community magazine. Appointment flow swings wildly.

Here's what the system looked like for him:

- **Message:** We sharpen their positioning to family-friendly clinic with same-day sick visits, fear-minimized handling, and strong dentistry and surgical capability.

- **Findability:** We optimize the Google Business Profile, add new service pages targeting top keywords, and update the website with 25 real photos of the team and facility. We humanize the brand.

- **Reviews engine:** The team asks at discharge; an SMS review link goes out automatically; QR standees go up at the front desk. Review volume triples in 60 days. Google ranking starts to climb.

- **Google Ads:** We launch campaigns on high-intent terms ("vet near me," "dog vomiting," "cat dental cleaning") with landing pages that show proof and a clear "Book Now" button.

- **Front desk training:** The team receives a speed-to-lead playbook with scenario-based role-play training. Median response time drops from hours to minutes.
- **Social media:** Real photos and practice updates are posted to Facebook and Instagram twice per week.

✓ ***In 90 days, cost per new client drops by 40%. Appointment variance narrows. Stress goes down.***

Scenario B: Equine and Farm Animal Practice (Semi-Rural)

Dr. Parker's practice is more active—three doctors, ten staff, and field service for sport horses and herd health. Competitors are regional and referral-driven.

- **Positioning:** We refine the messaging around rapid-response farm calls, digital radiography on-site, and performance lameness expertise.

- **Website:** We update it to speak regionally and by discipline—barrel racing, hunter/jumper, dressage—with case-study proof and transport guidelines.

- **Referral Network:** We strengthen relationships with farriers and trainers through co-branded referral forms and fast consultation feedback loops.

- **Google Ads:** Regional campaigns target specific conditions and services, with call extensions and a "Text to Book Farm Call" option.
- **Routing and Capacity:** We install scheduling logic based on time windows, geographic clusters, and minimum call thresholds to keep efficiency high.
- **Social Media:** Posts feature on-site service and real updates from doctors after treatments. Real pictures and video—no stock, no generic graphics.

✓ ***Revenue grows through targeted cases, and mileage per revenue dollar improves.***

Scenario C: Large Small-Animal + Exotics Clinic in the City

Dr. Chen owns a five-doctor small animal and exotics practice in a major metro area. They're well known locally, but their marketing is scattered. Their website is full of stock photos, barely mentions exotics, and the phones stay jammed all day.

- **Message:** We sharpen positioning to "Expert Care for Dogs, Cats, and Exotics," with new species-specific service pages for rabbits, reptiles, and birds—plus real photos of the doctors handling exotic patients.
- **Content and Visuals:** We coordinate a photo and video shoot of the team at work. The website gets updated with engaging content that describes their actual services (not generic veterinary text) and showcases the upbeat culture of the clinic. Photos include real local clients and their pets to build inclusion and community connection.
- **Findability:** The Google Business Profile gets updated categories for exotic care, 20 new photos are uploaded, and SEO pages are added targeting terms like "exotic vet near me," "reptile vet [city]," and "rabbit vet [city]."

- **Reviews:** QR code signs go up in treatment rooms and reception, making it effortless to leave a review.
- **Google Ads:** Targeted campaigns for exotics and small animal preventive care, each leading to a clean landing page with trust-building proof and a clear "Book Now" button.
- **Front Desk:** The team receives a short intake script for both small animal and exotic inquiries, plus a speed-to-lead workflow that cuts response times dramatically.
- **Social Media:** The clinic posts real cases and behind-the-scenes content twice a week to build credibility.

✓ ***In 90 days, appointments surge, phone chaos drops, and the practice becomes the city's go-to clinic for both small animals and exotics.***

By the time you finish this book, you'll have:

- **A clear persona** of your ideal new client and how to reach them
- **A compelling value proposition** that differentiates you for the right reasons
- **A simple channel plan** that matches the intent of your ideal clients
- **A conversion playbook** for your front desk
- **A reviews engine** that compounds trust month after month
- **A social media presence** that builds community and keeps your practice top of mind
- **A retention program** that increases lifetime value without spamming your list

QUICK WINS YOU CAN IMPLEMENT THIS WEEK

Before we dive into the full system, here are five things you can do right now to start building momentum immediately.

1. Clarify The Promise On Your Homepage

Write one clear headline that states who you serve and what you're great at. For example:

- "Gentle, Same-Day Care for Dogs & Cats in [Your City]"
- "On-Farm Equine Care with Performance Lameness Expertise Across [Region]"
- "Your Local [City Name] Pet & Farm Animal Clinic"

2. Make Booking Obvious

Put "Book Now" or "Request Appointment" in the top-right corner of your navigation and as a prominent button on every service page. Add "Call" and "Text" options if possible. The ability to receive and respond to texts quickly is growing in importance every year.

3. Turn Happy Moments Into Reviews

Train your team to ask for a review during natural high points — healthy pet checkouts, successful surgeries, dental follow-ups. Put up QR code standees in treatment rooms and at the sign-out desk. Make it a habit, not an afterthought.

4. Claim And Optimize Your Google Business Profile

Make sure your hours, services, photos, and categories are accurate and up to date. Post 5–10 fresh photos this week: your team, lobby, exam rooms, and real patients with permission. Happy people and happy pets make your clinic look approachable and trustworthy.

5. Measure One Thing That Matters

Start tracking one simple weekly metric: **New Clients by Source.** Train your front desk to ask every new client how they found you — Google Search, Maps, Friend Referral, Drive-By, Social, or Ad. Keep a tally each week. Patterns will appear quickly, and you'll know exactly where to focus.

✓ ***These Five Actions*** *alone will create a noticeable lift within 30–60 days — and every bit of progress you make now will only be reinforced and amplified as we move deeper into the chapters ahead.*

In the next chapter, we'll define your ideal client personas in detail — by species, service line, and local context — so your message lands with the people most likely to become loyal, long-term clients. From there, we'll build your findability, your conversion path, and your retention engine step by step, until your practice runs on a stable foundation, powerful local trust, and a predictable new-client flow you can count on.

Take a breath.

I'm glad you're here.

Let's get started.

Chapter 2

UNDERSTANDING YOUR IDEAL CLIENT

"There is only one winning strategy. It is to carefully define the target market and direct a superior offering to that target market."

— Philip Kotler, Father of Modern Marketing

Before we can build a marketing system that consistently brings new clients through your doors, we first must get clear about who those clients are. Every successful marketing strategy — no matter the industry — begins with naming and understanding your target audience. Not just in broad categories like "pet owners." Most vets start there, and I get it — it's a fine place to begin. But then you've got to refine and define who your target audience really is. You need detailed, practical personas based on species, needs, behavior, and local context.

The more precisely you define who you're trying to reach, the easier it becomes to attract them.

Most veterinary practices skip this step. They start with the "pet owners" concept and leave it at that. Honestly, almost all business owners do at first. The thinking goes something like: "I help animals. If someone needs me, they'll find me." And maybe they will — for a while.

But here's what I've seen happen when practices market to everyone: the message gets blurred, the website sounds generic, and the ads attract the wrong people — or no one at all. You may get lucky with what's called "shotgun marketing" and see a few new faces come through the door. But over time, that approach wears you out, stresses your team, and drains your budget without building anything lasting. Your results with this approach are mediocre at best. The shift I'm asking you to make is this: stop chasing everyone and start attracting the right ones.

In this chapter, we'll pinpoint your ideal client personas — the dog owners looking for same-day sick care, the cat owners who value low-stress handling, the horse owners seeking specialized equine expertise, the farm clients needing dependable field service, and more. We'll break down what they care about, how they search, what influences their decisions, and how to speak directly to their motivations.

Once we nail down who you need to be talking to specifically, every part of your marketing becomes sharper, simpler, and more effective. Your website speaks directly to their concerns. Your ads attract the right people. Your reviews improve. And you come away with a bigger win — feeling like you're doing great work for the right people, who genuinely appreciate your practice.

Why the Wrong Clients Cost You More Than You Think

Veterinary practices don't fail because they lack clients — they struggle because they attract the wrong mix. Price-shoppers. Clients who don't follow treatment plans. Farm clients who cancel too often. Emergency-only visitors who never return and want services at times when you're not available. People who are difficult with your staff and drain morale without contributing to the health of your practice. You've probably experienced some of these.

When your marketing speaks directly to your best clients, two things happen: you attract more of the people who make your practice profitable, and you naturally reduce the number of clients who cost you time, money, and energy. Actually, there's a third thing that happens too — you and your staff have more fun, and morale stays consistently higher.

You probably don't have just one ideal client, you have a handful of primary segments. Your job isn't to guess them. It's to identify them clearly.

Common client groups in veterinary medicine include dog owners, cat owners, exotic pet owners, horse owners, and farm clients. Which of these groups do you want more of? Your answer to that question is the key. Don't try to attract all of them equally. Instead, focus on the clients who follow your recommendations, pay on time, respect your team, value your expertise, return year after year, and refer others just like them. But we're not finished yet — let's keep defining.

BUILDING YOUR CLIENT PERSONA

The next step is to build what's called a client persona — sometimes referred to as a target audience "avatar." A persona is a clear, usable snapshot of your ideal client. It should not be a three-page fantasy profile. It should answer four simple questions:

What do they want?

What do they worry about?

How do they search?

What helps them choose?

That's it. Keep it practical and you'll actually use it.

When you're ready to build your own, turn to Appendix A — Ideal Client Persona Builder at the back of this book, or visit cebronwalker.com and download the form under the Free Resources tab. It walks you through a simple survey and worksheet, one persona at a time, so you come away with a clear, actionable profile you can hand to your team and plug directly into your marketing.

The Five Core Veterinary Client Personas

Here are five of the most common client personas in veterinary medicine. As you read through them, think about which one, or which combination, best represents the clients your practice most wants to attract.

Persona 1: The Dog Owner with a Sick Pet

- Primary need: Fast care, clear diagnosis, transparent next steps
- Search behavior: "Vet near me," "dog vomiting," "my dog won't eat," "same-day vet"
- Booking behavior: Wants online booking, helpful web chat, and/or a fast phone response
- Decision factors: Reviews, availability, clarity, compassion
- Key message: *"Same-day care you can trust when your dog needs help now."*

Persona 2: The Cat Owner Who Values Low Stress

- Primary need: Calm environment, gentle handling
- Search behavior: "Cat-friendly vet," "fear-free vet," "low-stress cat vet"
- Booking behavior: Schedules in advance, prefers consistency
- Decision factors: Trust, handling philosophy, quiet waiting area, real photos and videos, human-centered social media
- Key message: *"Gentle, feline-friendly care that reduces stress for both of you."*

Persona 3: The Exotic Pet Owner Seeking Expertise

- Primary need: A veterinarian who actually knows their species

- Search behavior: "Bearded dragon vet near me," "rabbit vet," "avian vet [city]"
- Booking behavior: Schedules in advance, prefers consistency
- Decision factors: Trust, handling philosophy, quiet waiting area, real photos and videos, human-centered social media
- Key message: *"Gentle, feline-friendly care that reduces stress for both of you."*

Persona 4: The Equine Owner Who Needs Reliability

- Primary need: Quick response times and confidence in lameness or emergency care
- Search behavior: Rarely Google — typically referrals, word-of-mouth, and human-centered social media stories and videos
- Booking behavior: Prefers text and personal connection
- Decision factors: Experience, availability, reputation within discipline communities, social media presence
- Key message: *"Expert on-farm equine care with dependable scheduling."*

Persona 5: The Farm Client Needing Routine and Emergency Care

- Primary need: Herd health, predictable schedules, emergency readiness
- Search behavior: Local reputation carries more weight than online search
- Booking behavior: Direct phone — rarely online forms
- Decision factors: Reliability, service area, pricing clarity, social media that showcases real farm services
- Key message: *"Expert on-farm equine care with dependable scheduling."*

Pick the persona, or the combination of a couple, that best fits your practice. You'll immediately start to see how your marketing could be sharpened to speak directly to those clients.

HOW YOUR IDEAL CLIENT FINDS YOU: THE BUYER'S JOURNEY

Once you've identified who your ideal clients are, the next question is: how do they find you? Each persona follows a similar path from need to booked appointment. We call this the buyer's journey, and it moves through four stages: Awareness, Discovery, Evaluation, and Decision.

Missing clarity at any one of these stages can cost you a new client — not because you weren't the right fit, but because something in the process let them slip away to another clinic.

Here's how each stage works in the real world of veterinary marketing.

Awareness

This is the moment a need appears. Their dog is limping. Their cat stopped eating. Their horse is off. They are suddenly, urgently aware that they need help. This is where your marketing journey with them begins — even before they know your name.

Discovery

Now they go looking. This might be a Google search, Google Maps, a local Facebook group where they ask for recommendations, a referral from a friend, or a social media post that catches their eye. Some will open ChatGPT and ask about treatment options or local practice recommendations based on reviews. This is where your visibility — your findability — either puts you in front of them or leaves you invisible.

AI Is Now Part of the Buyer's Journey

Something new has entered the discovery phase — **and it's moving fast.** A growing number of pet owners are turning to AI tools like ChatGPT, Google Gemini, and others to research symptoms, ask questions about their pet's health, and even get recommendations on local veterinary practices. They're asking things like: *"What are the best-reviewed veterinary clinics near me that see exotic pets?"* or *"My dog has been vomiting — what should I do and where should I go?"*

This matters for your practice in two important ways.

First, AI tools pull from publicly available information — including your Google reviews, your website content, and your overall online presence. The stronger and clearer your digital footprint, the more likely you are to show up favorably when AI makes a recommendation. Second, when a potential client arrives at your website after an AI interaction, much of the evaluation has already happened. They may already be leaning toward booking — which means your job is simply to make that final step as easy as possible.

You don't need to become an AI expert. You need to make sure the basics are done well — and that's exactly what this book will show you.

Evaluation

They've found you. Now they're sizing you up. They read your reviews. They look at your photos. They scroll your social media to see if your practice feels like a place they can trust. They visit your website to see if you handle their specific animal or situation. If they found you through an AI tool like ChatGPT, the evaluation may have already happened before they landed on your page. Either way, at the end of this stage they're asking themselves one quiet question: Are you actually the right fit for me and my pet?

Decision

They've decided they like you. Now you just need to make it easy to say yes. A clear "Book Now" button. A friendly voice on the phone. A front desk team that's warm, efficient, and confident. This is where the appointment is won or lost — not by your clinical skills, but by how frictionless and welcoming that final step feels.

SPEAK YOUR IDEAL CLIENT'S LANGUAGE

Now that you know who your ideal clients are and how they find you, the next step is making sure your message meets them where they are — across every channel you use to reach them, whether that's your website, social media, email, or ads.

Here's something worth remembering: your clients think in outcome language, not medical terminology. They aren't searching for "feline hyperthyroidism management." They're searching for "why is my cat losing weight." They aren't thinking about "preventive dental prophylaxis." They're thinking, "I don't want my dog's breath to smell like that."

Speak their language and your message lands. Speak yours and they keep scrolling.

Here's what that looks like in practice across three common personas. Pay close attention here — you'll see right away how you can improve the way you write and speak, whether that's on your website, your social media, or even over the phone with a potential new client.

Persona 1: The Dog Owner with a Sick Pet

Generic message: "Our clinic provides comprehensive small animal veterinary services including diagnostics, surgery, and preventive care."

Persona-targeted message: "When your dog isn't acting right, you need answers fast — not a two-week wait. We offer same-day sick visits so you can get your dog seen, diagnosed, and on the road to feeling better today."

What changed: The targeted version speaks to urgency, emotion, and a specific outcome. It answers the client's real fear — Will I have to wait while my dog suffers? — before they even ask it.

Persona 2: The Cat Owner Who Values Low Stress

Generic message: "We welcome cats and dogs and offer a full range of feline health services."

Persona-targeted message: "We know bringing your cat to the vet can be stressful — for both of you. Our fear-free spaces are designed just for cats, with quieter waiting areas, gentler handling, and a team that truly understands feline behavior. Because your cat deserves care that doesn't feel like a battle."

What changed: The targeted version acknowledges the client's specific anxiety — the stress of the vet visit itself — and positions your handling philosophy as the solution. It builds trust before the first appointment is even booked.

Persona 3: The Exotic Pet Owner Seeking Expertise

Generic message: "Our experienced veterinary team is here to care for all your pets."

Persona-targeted message: "Rabbits, reptiles, and birds have unique health needs that most general practices aren't equipped to handle. Our team has hands-on experience with exotic species — so when your bearded dragon stops eating or your rabbit needs a check-up, you're not guessing whether we know what we're doing. You already know."

What changed: The targeted version directly addresses the exotic owner's biggest fear — finding a vet who actually knows their animal. It establishes species-specific credibility immediately, which is exactly what this high-intent client is looking for before they ever pick up the phone.

The pattern is the same every time. Find the real fear or desire behind the need. Name it plainly. Then show how your practice solves it — in their words, not yours.

Your ideal clients keep coming back, are more appreciative — which makes all the difference — spend more over the lifetime of their animal, and refer others just like them. When you target these people effectively, your cost of effort goes down and your results go up. You spend less on ads for more qualified leads. Your social posts need to be fewer but better. Your website converts faster and more easily.

In the next chapter, we'll take your client personas and use them to build the cornerstone of your marketing — your message. You'll learn how to clearly articulate what makes your practice different in a way that resonates deeply with your ideal clients and positions you distinctly in your local market.

This is where your marketing starts becoming magnetic.

Chapter Three

MESSAGE-MARKET FIT

"1,000 Songs in Your Pocket."

— Steve Jobs, introducing the iPod

Marketing Is a Communication Art

No matter how advanced your tools become, no matter how many platforms emerge or disappear, one truth remains constant: clients choose the business whose message feels like it's speaking directly to them.

When Steve Jobs stood before 300 Apple employees and members of the press at his now-famous iPod unveiling, he didn't lead with technical specifications or manufacturing milestones. He led with a single, clear, human sentence. He knew exactly who his audience was, what they wanted, and what would move them. The rest, as they say, is history.

In the previous chapter, we clarified who your ideal clients are and what they care about. Now let's take that understanding and turn it into a message that resonates — instantly, emotionally, and clearly.

This is where many veterinary practices stumble. They try to speak to everyone, and in doing so, they dilute their communication — getting new business by chance, not by intention.

Let's be frank. You probably speak beautifully to your clients about their pets in the exam room. You know exactly what to say without even thinking about it. If we had a camera on you in there, you'd look and sound like the most confident, knowledgeable vet in the world. But veterinary medicine is full of talented clinicians who communicate perfectly in exam rooms and struggle to express that same value in the public marketplace. When the camera turns on you for that perfect social video, you might just go blank. Am I right?

You and your team were trained to speak in medical terms — not in client language. Meanwhile, your ideal clients are regular, non-medical people who are searching online, comparing options, reading reviews, and asking themselves questions they may never say out loud: *"Does this clinic understand my pet?" "Can I trust these people?" "Will they take care of us if something goes wrong?" "Is this the right place for my animal or will I just be treated like a number?"*

Your job is to answer those questions — in plain, warm, human language — through your website, your social media, your videos, and your blogs. That's the art of marketing. That's what good messaging does. When we talk about "magnetic messaging," we mean the kind of communication that transforms a hesitant pet owner into a booked appointment. This is how your clinic stands out in a crowded field — especially against the bigger corporate clinics with the larger ad budgets.

When your message fits your market, it creates a sense of recognition and trust that no discount, coupon, or gimmick can match.

THE ROLE OF AI IN CRAFTING MAGNETIC MESSAGES

For the first time in history, you have access to AI tools like ChatGPT and others that can help you shape, refine, and test your messaging with extraordinary speed and clarity.

Kurt Allen, Vice President of Marketing and Communications at Notre Dame de Namur University and a Forbes Communications Council member, captures this well. Writing in Forbes, Allen argues that enduring marketing isn't built on trends — it's built on truth. "Staying true to the brand's voice and purpose," he writes, "builds trust, fosters connection and creates long-term impact beyond fleeting trends."[1] That principle applies directly to your practice. When your messaging reflects who you genuinely are and who you authentically serve, it resonates in a way no ad budget can manufacture.

AI won't replace your judgment or the heart behind your words — and it certainly won't replace you — but it can dramatically accelerate your ability to communicate with precision.

AI can help you:

- Translate complex medical explanations into simple, client-friendly language
- Generate headline variations based on what different client personas respond to
- Test whether your email, blog, or social post would be clear and understandable to the average pet owner
- Brainstorm positioning ideas that differentiate your clinic authentically
- Analyze your competitors' messaging so you can stand apart
- Write new web pages for a service in a warmer, more compassionate tone — tailored to your target audience
- Ensure your message directly addresses the fears, needs, or hopes of a specific client type

Think of AI as a messaging assistant, not an author. It can surface insights, summarize themes, and offer options — but the heart, integrity, and personality of your clinic must always come from you.

In the chapters ahead, you'll see exactly how to use AI to support and improve your marketing with accuracy and brand consistency. For now, simply understand this: your message becomes magnetic when it reflects the truth of who you are, the clarity of who you serve, and the confidence of someone who genuinely understands their clients. AI just helps you express that truth more quickly and more clearly.

As we work through this chapter, you'll learn how to articulate a message that answers the three silent questions every prospective client is asking: What makes this practice unique? Do their values align with mine? And — are they the right clinic for me and my pet?

Message–Market Fit

Before you can create messaging that consistently attracts the right clients, you need to understand the concept at the heart of all effective marketing: Message–Market Fit.

Message–Market Fit simply means that the words you use match the expectations, needs, and emotional state of the clients you want to attract. When your message fits, everything becomes easier — clients understand you faster, trust you sooner, and book appointments with less hesitation. When your message doesn't fit, even the best clinic in town can struggle to convert new clients.

Veterinarians might assume clients choose a practice based on credentials, equipment, or clinical skill. You'd be wrong. Clients take for granted that you're a competent veterinarian — that's the baseline. What they're actually evaluating is something deeper. After working with veterinary clinics for many years, I can tell you with confidence: the practices that don't take their clients for granted, and who work intentionally to make sure their messaging fits, win the business. Consistently.

Here's the important thing to get your head around: new clients make decisions based on human values — reassurance, relatability, clarity, and trust. They choose the practice that makes them feel seen and understood, sometimes without even being able to explain why. Translate that understanding through your website, your social media, and every message that goes out to the public — and you're golden.

A quick review of veterinary websites will show you that most clinics unintentionally sound the same. Warm, well-meaning phrases like "quality care," "compassionate service," and "treating your pets like family" appear everywhere — usually sitting above stock photos of puppies and kittens. This creates a fog of sameness that makes it nearly impossible for clients to tell one clinic from another.

That's where differentiation comes in.

WHAT ACTUALLY MAKES YOU DIFFERENT

This is one of the most misunderstood concepts in veterinary marketing — and one of the most important. So before we go any further, let's talk about it directly.

Many practices believe differentiation means being better: better medicine, better equipment, better service, better outcomes. The problem is that "better" is almost impossible for a prospective client to recognize online — especially in the few seconds they spend scanning a website, a Google listing, or a social post. When every clinic claims to be compassionate, experienced, and high-quality, those claims begin to cancel each other out.

In his book Get Different, marketing expert Mike Michalowicz puts this reality into sharp focus. He argues that in marketing, "Better is not better. Different is better." His point isn't that quality doesn't matter — it absolutely does — but that uncommunicated quality looks identical to average quality. As Michalowicz explains, businesses stall not because they lack competence, but because they fail to create clear, effective differentiation. In his words, "The lack of marketing — good, effective, different marketing — is the driving reason for small business mediocrity and stunted growth."

This challenge shows up clearly in veterinary medicine. Most clinics are good. Many are excellent. Yet to a searching pet owner, they often sound interchangeable. Trying to be "better" forces clients into comparison — Who's really better? How would I even know? — which creates hesitation and slows decisions. Being different, on the other hand, creates recognition.

Michalowicz explains that our brains are wired for efficiency. We skim. We filter. We conserve energy. We only stop scrolling when something stands out as unfamiliar, relevant, or unexpected. Being different doesn't mean flashy or extreme. It means distinct — and immediately understandable to the right person.

Consider a few examples:

- **A feline-only clinic** that leads with calm, low-stress handling and a cat-centric environment isn't claiming superior medicine. It's declaring relevance.
- **An equine practice** that emphasizes rapid response times and reliability isn't louder — it's clearer.
- **A general practice** that consistently offers same-day sick appointments differentiates through availability, not bravado.
- **An exotics clinic** stands out simply by confidently naming the species it knows best.

None of these practices are shouting. They're simply specific.

This is where differentiation and Message–Market Fit intersect. Differentiation gives your messaging traction. It tells the right client — this is for you — before they ever read deeply. And here's something important to understand: differentiation doesn't exclude people arbitrarily. It filters. It invites the clients you serve best to lean in, while quietly allowing others to self-select out. That clarity makes your marketing calmer, more ethical, and more effective.

Once your differentiation is clear, your messaging stops competing for attention and begins creating connection.

Your Best Messages Are Already Inside Your Practice

Here's the good news: you don't have to invent your differentiation from scratch. It's already there. It lives in the conversations you have every day — with the worried caller, the new puppy parent, the lifelong client who trusts every recommendation, the cat owner who appreciates gentle handling, the equine client who values reliability above everything else.

Start by listening to what your clients repeatedly say:

- *"I just want someone who will explain things clearly."*
- *"I need a vet who won't judge me."*
- *"I need to know I can get in quickly when something happens."*
- *"I need someone who actually understands exotics."*
- *"I want a place my cat won't panic."*
- *"I need someone dependable for farm calls."*

These aren't marketing slogans — they're signals. They tell you exactly what matters most to the people you want more of. When you or your marketing team write your messaging, write with these voices in mind. Speak to their hopes, their fears, their frustrations, and their expectations.

The Best Marketing Insights Come From Your Own Clients

Before you write a single word of website copy or record your first social media video, try this: listen. Really listen to what your clients say — not just when they compliment you, but when they explain why they came to you, what they were worried about, and what made them feel relieved. Those words are marketing gold.

Here are the kinds of things veterinary clients say every day — and what they're really telling you:

- *"I just want someone who will explain things clearly."* → They've felt talked down to or confused before. Clarity is your differentiator.
- *"I need a vet who won't judge me."* → They feel vulnerable about their pet's care. Compassion without judgment is your differentiator.
- *"I need to know I can get in quickly when something happens."* → Availability and responsiveness are your differentiators.
- *"I need someone who actually understands exotics."* → Expertise and specificity are your differentiators.
- *"I want a place my cat won't panic."* → Environment and handling philosophy are your differentiators.
- *"I need someone dependable for farm calls."* → Reliability and consistency are your differentiators.

Start collecting these phrases from your own clients. Ask your front desk team what callers say most often. Read your own Google reviews and write down the exact words your happiest clients use. Then use those words — not your words — in your marketing.

That's not copying. That's listening.

This is also why client testimonials — featured prominently on your website, ideally as short videos — are so powerful. Your best messaging often comes straight from the mouths of your happiest clients. What they say about you is what makes you different. Let them say it for you.

Your differentiation might come from any of the following:

- **Your approach**: low-stress handling, longer appointments, radical transparency
- **Your availability**: same-day sick visits, extended hours, emergency access
- **Your species expertise**: exotics, equine, feline-only care
- **Your equipment**: advanced diagnostics, imaging, dental capabilities
- **Your philosophy:** relationship-based medicine, continuity of care
- **Your environment**: quiet cat rooms, modern design, large-animal facilities
- **Your team**: specialized interests, certifications, emergency experience

Differentiation doesn't need to be dramatic. It just needs to be clear. A feline-only practice differentiates by creating a calm, cat-centric experience. An equine vet differentiates by being consistently available and responsive. An exotics vet differentiates by emphasizing rare species expertise.

You can differentiate through values, tone, or personality. You can differentiate through consistency and reliability. You can differentiate by simply explaining what you believe in — clearly. The goal is to help the right clients understand, without hesitation, why your practice is their practice.

CRAFTING YOUR CORE MESSAGE

Every strong marketing system is built on one central message — a simple, memorable statement that communicates who you serve, what you offer, and why it matters.

Your core message is not your slogan. It is the spine of your entire communication. It shapes your website headlines, your Google listing, your ads, your emails, your social posts, and the way your front desk speaks on the phone. It should be immediately understandable — even at a glance. Here are a few examples written to reflect strong Message–Market Fit:

- *"Same-day care when your dog needs help fast."*
- *"Gentle, feline-friendly handling that reduces stress for both of you."*
- *"Experienced care for reptiles, rabbits, and birds."*
- *"Reliable on-farm equine care with rapid response times."*
- *"Preventive care that keeps your pet healthy year-round."*

These messages work because they speak directly to a specific client with a specific need. They don't try to be everything to everyone. And if your practice does serve several of these client types, that's perfectly fine — you can have different web pages, different social posts, and different ad campaigns that each apply the right message to the right audience.

Write Your Own Core Message

Grab yourself a pencil for this one — you'll want to be able to erase and adjust as you go.

Using the examples above as a guide, write your own core message in the space below. Remember — it should be one clear sentence that speaks directly to your ideal client, names what you offer, and tells them why it matters.

Keep it simple. Keep it specific. Keep it human.

My practice serves: ______________________________

What we do best: ______________________________

Why it matters to them: ______________________________

My core message: ______________________________

____

____

Now test it. Ask yourself:

- Does it speak directly to one specific type of client?
- Would a pet owner understand it instantly — without any veterinary knowledge?
- Does it tell them something meaningful about why your practice is different?

If you answered yes to all three — you've got your core message. If not, try again. It often takes two or three passes to get it right, and that's perfectly normal.

Using AI to Refine Your Message

Once you have a draft message, AI can be a genuinely useful tool for sharpening it. Many veterinarians find it helpful to paste a draft into an AI tool and ask:

- *"Rewrite this so the average pet owner understands it instantly."*
- *"Make this sound calmer and more reassuring."*
- *"Does this message speak to a cat owner? Why or why not?"*

AI will not replace your voice — but it will help you polish it. It's not cheating. It's using modern tools to get clearer about who you are, who you serve, and how to reach them. The goal has always been the same: help the right clients find the right doctor to keep their animals healthy and happy. AI just helps you get there faster.

Your Message, Your Story, Your Difference

When you understand your ideal clients and speak to them clearly, every other part of your marketing system becomes stronger. Your ads become more effective. Your website converts more visitors. Your reviews begin to align with your brand. Your front desk feels more confident. And clients arrive already trusting you — before they ever walk through the door.

That's the power of getting your message right. And that's exactly what we've been building toward.

In the next chapter, we'll move into findability — making sure the right clients can actually find you when they're searching. Because even the most magnetic message in the world only works if the right people get to see it.

Footnote:

[1] Kurt Allen, "20 Timeless Principles To Guide Your Marketing Approach," *Forbes Communications Council,* Forbes, August 21, 2025. *https://www.forbes.com/councils/forbescommunicationscouncil/2025/08/21/20-timeless-principles-to-guide-your-marketing-approach/*

PART TWO

MARKETING SYSTEMS

Building Trust, Expanding Reach & Accelerating New Client Acquisition

Chapter Four

LOCAL SEARCH, GOOGLE & AI

"76% of people who search for something nearby visit a business within a day. If you're not optimizing for local intent, you're leaving serious money on the table."

— Neil Patel, Bestselling Author and SEO Expert

Before a client ever calls your clinic, fills out a form, or taps "Book Now," something else happens — something small, silent, and absolutely decisive: they search.

"We're not getting found. We're not coming up," Dr. Kathryn told me during our very first call. "I need you to help me put my practice on the map." Aspen Veterinary Clinic in Spring Creek, Nevada was struggling with exactly that. Despite providing outstanding medicine — with clients who genuinely loved the care they received — the clinic's digital presence wasn't keeping pace with the quality of their work. Their website was outdated and hard to navigate. Social media happened only when someone could get to it, which wasn't often. And they had no local digital advertising whatsoever.

We got to work immediately. Day one, we addressed the Google Business Profile. From there came a new logo, a complete website rebuild, professional video production, social media management, and targeted Google and Facebook advertising. Not one thing in isolation — the full system, working together.

The results were significant. Within a few months of launching the plan, Aspen saw a 172% increase in new clients —

more than double the new client volume they had before. Their social media reach grew from roughly three people per day to over 2,000. Page impressions increased by 4,184%. Engagements were up 1,966%. Website clicks climbed 2,573%. And their follower base grew by 29% — with net new followers up 1,179%.

These weren't vanity numbers. They were the direct result of building a complete, consistent digital presence — one that made it easy for the right clients in Spring Creek to find Aspen, trust what they saw, and book an appointment.

Dr. Kathryn's practice was already excellent. The marketing just made sure the community could finally see it.

For years, "search" happened almost exclusively on Google. Today it still does — but Google is no longer the only place clients are turning for answers. Increasingly, pet owners are asking AI tools like ChatGPT, Google Gemini, Perplexity, and others to recommend local veterinarians, interpret symptoms, or point them toward help when something feels wrong.

In real time, these tools scan the web, summarize information, compare clinics, and present answers as if speaking with authority. Whether your clinic appears in those answers depends entirely on the digital footprint you've built.

This means your visibility must now operate on two fronts:

- **Human searchers** — worried, rushed, emotional, scanning for reassurance
- **AI search systems** (ChatGPT, Perplexity, Google Gemini) — tools that evaluate clarity, consistency, credibility, and publicly available information at scale

If Google can't clearly understand who you are, neither can AI. If your website, listings, or reviews are inconsistent, AI tools will rank or describe you inaccurately. If your messaging is unclear, AI can't summarize it well — and that costs you potential clients.

Visibility precedes choice. Clarity precedes trust. And trust precedes booking.

While this chapter is about being found, it's important to understand that today your website must be built not only to show up in Google searches, but also to be referenced accurately when AI tools like ChatGPT are asked for local recommendations. These are now two equally important goals.

Veterinary marketing often begins with ads or social media — but that's not where the client's journey begins. It begins with a typed or spoken question:

- *"Vet near me for a vomiting dog."*
- *"Best exotic vet in town."*
- *"Horse vet who does farm calls."*
- *"Cat-friendly veterinarian."*
- *"Sick rabbit won't eat — what do I do?"*

Your ability to appear in those answers is directly tied to how well you've structured your online presence. Local SEO is not about chasing algorithms or tricks. It's about helping both Google and AI systems understand the fundamentals about you and your clinic — who you are, where you are, what you treat, how you help, and why clients should trust you. When the digital world understands this clearly and consistently, you become findable. And when clients understand it, you become their choice.

In this chapter, we'll break down the four pillars of findability:

First, your online foundation — the accuracy of your name, address, phone number, and listings across the internet. These are the signals Google and AI use to verify your legitimacy.

Second, your Google Business Profile — the modern digital front door of your practice. For many clients, this is the first and sometimes only page they see before calling.

Third, your service pages and content — the species-specific, symptom-specific, and problem-specific pages that tell both humans and AI exactly what you do.

Fourth, your AI visibility — the specific signals that determine whether your clinic appears when pet owners ask ChatGPT or Google Gemini for a local recommendation.

Think of your online presence the same way you think of preventive care: small, consistent actions that keep your practice healthy, visible, and trusted over time.

You've clarified your message. Now let's make sure the world can find it — whether they're searching with their fingertips or asking an AI for a recommendation.

THE FOUR PILLARS OF BEING FOUND

Local visibility is built on a structure — four interconnected pillars that support every other marketing effort you make. When these pillars are strong, your clinic becomes easy to find, easy to trust, and easy to choose. When even one is weak, you can slip beneath the radar without ever realizing it.

Let's look at each one in a way that's simple, practical, and focused on what truly matters.

Pillar 1: Your Online Foundation - The Web's Confidence in You

Before any search platform can recommend your clinic, it needs to know who you are — with certainty. This happens long before rankings, reviews, or content come into play. It begins with the most basic identifying details of your business: your name, your address, your phone number, your hours, and your website.

These may seem simple, but they're incredibly powerful. Every time your clinic appears online — whether on Google, Facebook, Yelp, Apple Maps, or a veterinary directory — your information becomes part of a web-wide fingerprint. When that fingerprint is consistent, your clinic appears trustworthy and well-established. When it's inconsistent, search systems hesitate. They show your clinic less often, rank you lower, or suggest your competitors instead.

A clean, consistent foundation sends a clear signal: *"This is who we are. This is where we are. This is how clients reach us."*

That clarity alone can elevate your discoverability more than most people realize.

Pillar 2: Your Google Business Profile - Your Digital Front Door

Long before a pet owner steps through your physical front door, they step through your digital one. Today, that door is your Google Business Profile.

This single profile is often the very first interaction a potential client has with your clinic. It's the listing they see on Google Maps. It's the card that appears when someone searches "vet near me." It's the quick snapshot they use to decide whether to call you or keep scrolling.

In many cases, pet owners never even visit your website

before choosing a veterinarian. They rely entirely on what they see in your Google listing: reviews, photos, services, hours, and the general sense of activity and professionalism. A complete, well-maintained profile builds immediate confidence. An outdated or incomplete one sends clients elsewhere — quietly, and without explanation.

Your Google Business Profile is more than a listing. It's your first impression, your reputation center, your mini-website, and your most important local marketing tool — all wrapped into one.

When you keep your profile updated, add fresh photos regularly, respond to reviews, and present your services clearly, you're effectively greeting every potential client with a smile, a handshake, and a sense of welcome — all before they've ever made contact. I've included a quick-action checklist at the end of this chapter to help you improve your profile immediately.

Pillar 3: Your Service Pages - Clarity About What You Actually Do

The third pillar of findability is your website's structure — specifically the pages that explain your services. These pages are the bridge between a searcher's question and your clinic's solution.

Pet owners rarely search in general terms anymore. They search for specifics:

- *"Dog dental cleaning near me"*
- *"Cat vomiting but still eating"*
- *"Rabbit vet near me"*
- *"Pet X-ray in Nashville"*

If your website doesn't clearly address these needs, search platforms won't show your clinic as a relevant match — no matter how experienced or capable you are.

Service pages exist to remove that ambiguity. They tell both humans and search systems exactly what you treat, who you treat, and how you help. When done well, they act like beacons — drawing in the right cases, answering questions before they're asked, and reassuring anxious pet owners that they've found the right place.

Good service pages don't need to be complicated. They simply need to be clear. They explain conditions, outline your process, demonstrate expertise, and offer guidance. They help pet owners feel understood — and ready to take the next step. At the bottom of each service page, include a short set of Frequently Asked Questions — three to five common questions with straightforward answers. These FAQs serve both the reader who wants quick clarity and the search systems that reward thorough, helpful content.

When your service pages are complete, well-structured, and easy to navigate, they become one of your most powerful tools for both findability and client conversion.

Pillar 4: AI Visibility - Being Found When Clients Ask ChatGPT

This is new territory. And it matters more every month.

A growing number of pet owners are no longer starting their search on Google. They're opening ChatGPT, Claude, Grok, Google Gemini, Perplexity, or another AI tool and asking questions directly — questions like "What's the best veterinary clinic near me for exotic pets?" or "My dog has been vomiting all morning — what should I do and where should I go?"

These AI tools don't show a list of search results. They give a single, confident answer. And the clinics that appear in those answers aren't necessarily the ones with the biggest ad budgets. They're the ones whose digital presence is the clearest, most consistent, and most complete.

Here's how AI search tools decide who to recommend:

they scan publicly available information — your website content, your Google reviews, your business listings, your social media, and the overall clarity of your online presence. They're looking for signals that tell them: this clinic is legitimate, well-reviewed, clearly described, and relevant to this specific question. The stronger those signals, the more likely you are to show up in an AI-generated recommendation.

The good news is that AI visibility is not a separate system you need to build from scratch. It is a direct byproduct of doing the first three pillars well. A consistent online foundation, a complete and active Google Business Profile, and clear service pages all feed directly into how AI tools understand and represent your practice.

That said, there are a few specific things worth paying attention to as AI search becomes more prominent:

- **Clarity of language on your website:** AI tools summarize what they find. If your website is vague, generic, or full of medical jargon, AI can't summarize you accurately or compellingly. Write your service pages and homepage in plain, specific, client-friendly language — the same language we covered in Chapter 3.

- **Google reviews volume and recency:** AI tools weigh reviews heavily when making local recommendations. A clinic with 200 recent, detailed reviews is far more likely to be referenced than one with 40 old ones. We'll cover your reviews engine in depth in the next chapter.

- **Consistent name, address, and phone across all platforms**: AI tools cross-reference your information across multiple sources. Inconsistencies create uncertainty, and uncertain information gets left out of recommendations.

- **Species and service specificity:** If you treat exotics, say so clearly and repeatedly across your website, your Google profile, and your content. AI tools match questions to answers.

The more specifically you describe what you do, the more accurately you get matched to the clients asking for it.

A Note on AI Search Optimization (ASO)

Beyond the content and clarity improvements above, there is now an additional layer of technical infrastructure worth knowing about — one that most veterinary websites don't yet have in place.

Traditional SEO helps your website show up on Google. But AI systems look for something different. They need clear, well-organized, machine-readable information that helps them understand who you are, what you do, and why your practice matters. Many existing websites — even well-designed ones — are difficult for AI systems to interpret correctly. They may be overlooked, misunderstood, or only partially understood when an AI tool goes looking for a local recommendation.

AI Search Optimization, or ASO, is a behind-the-scenes infrastructure layer applied to your website that helps AI systems discover it, understand it more clearly, and reference it with greater confidence. This includes creating special discovery files and structured website signals, organizing content so automated systems receive cleaner information, and tracking real AI crawler activity on your site so you can see exactly which AI systems are visiting and what they're accessing.

Think of it this way: SEO gets you found by Google. ASO gets you found — and understood — by AI. **You need both.**

This is not a replacement for your existing SEO or content strategy. It's an additional layer of infrastructure that prepares your website for the way modern discovery is evolving. And the practices that put this in place now will have a meaningful head start on the ones that wait.

If you'd like to explore what ASO looks like for your specific practice, visit **walkerkreative.com/ai-search-optimization**, or ask your current marketing provider whether your website is currently optimized for AI discovery.

This is genuinely new territory in veterinary marketing — and most practices aren't paying attention to it yet. That makes it one of the most significant opportunities available to you right now.

You don't need to become an AI expert. You need to make sure your digital presence is clear, consistent, complete, and human. The rest follows naturally.

Bringing It All Together

These four pillars — your foundational listings, your Google Business Profile, your service pages, and your AI visibility — create a complete ecosystem of findability. They work quietly in the background, guiding anxious pet owners toward your clinic at the exact moment they need you most.

When they are strong, you rise above the noise. When they are neglected, even excellent clinics disappear from view.

Make it easy for your community to find you. That is the true heart of local SEO.

TOOLS & QUICK WINS FOR THE PRACTICE OWNER

To make this chapter immediately practical, here are three simple actions you can take right now — no technical skills required.

1. Run a Digital Footprint Audit

Search your clinic name on Google and look at every listing that appears. As you go, ask yourself:

- Is the clinic name spelled consistently across all listings?
- Is the phone number the same everywhere?
- Are any old addresses still showing up?
- Are your hours accurate and up to date?

Correct anything that's outdated or inconsistent. This single step can meaningfully improve how search systems interpret and rank your practice.

2. Add Three New Photos to Your Google Business Profile

Clients love visuals — and fresh photos also improve your profile's visibility in search. Upload at least three this week:

- A smiling team member holding a patient
- A bright, clean exam room
- The exterior of your clinic with clear, readable signage

3. Update Your Service List on Google

Many clinics overlook this entirely. Log into your Google Business Profile and add or refine your services to include specifics such as:

- Dentistry
- Spay/neuter
- Cold laser therapy
- Ultrasound
- Exotic care

The more clearly your services are listed, the more relevant searches your clinic will appear in.

BEFORE YOU MOVE ON – A QUICK CHECKLIST

The three quick wins above are a strong start, but there's a more complete action list waiting for you. The full Local SEO & AI Visibility Checklist for Veterinary Practices covers everything in this chapter in a simple, step-by-step format you can hand directly to your team or work through yourself in an afternoon. It includes:

- A full digital footprint audit walkthrough
- Google Business Profile optimization steps
- Service page structure guidelines
- AI visibility checklist items specific to veterinary websites

Grab it free at **cebronwalker.com/free-resources** or scan the QR code below.

Scan Me!

In the next chapter, we move into one of the most powerful trust-building tools your practice has — your Google reviews and online reputation. Because once clients can find you, the next question they ask is: Can I trust you? That's exactly what we'll help you answer.

Chapter Five

BECOMING THE BEST CHOICE

"The whole point of marketing is one thing: to gain trust. Because once someone trusts you, you don't need to do anything else besides keep it."

— Alex Hormozi, Bestselling Author

Consumers no longer take a brand's word for it — they look for proof. Scott Baradell, author of *Trust Signals: Brand Building in a Post-Truth World*, defines trust signals as "clues or evidence that help people feel confident in a decision" — the reviews, testimonials, awards, and third-party validations that reassure buyers they're making the right choice.

As Baradell puts it, when a trusted third party vouches for your brand, it says more than any ad campaign ever could. Trust isn't something a brand can claim — it's something others must confirm. Reviews and endorsements provide that confirmation.

So, before you run ads or invest in an expensive social media campaign, ask yourself: do you have the reviews and trust signals in place that will convert curious visitors into booked appointments?

Let me tell you about my friend Monique.

Many years ago in Sacramento, Monique wanted to take her passion for fitness out of her garage and into a real CrossFit studio. I designed her a logo, built her a website, launched her social channels, and she signed up her first group of clients — my wife and I included. Monique was an exceptional coach. Her technical knowledge of fitness and movement was extraordinary. But beyond our group of fifteen clients, nobody in town knew she existed.

The turning point came when we focused on trust signals. I got that small group of clients to leave reviews, share their own social videos about her classes, and talk openly about the results they were getting. User-generated content — real people, real results, real voices — started doing what no ad could.

Soon she doubled her clients. By the end of the year, she had outgrown her space and moved into a new building. She's never needed to run ads.

But here's what made her growth truly remarkable — it wasn't just the number of new clients. It was the quality of them. The UGC and social proof she had built expanded her value and reach across the community in ways that attracted entirely different types of clients than she expected. A retired multimillionaire found her through the buzz and hired her for personal coaching — he wanted to stay in peak physical shape as he aged and wasn't going to trust just anyone with that. A wave of young women followed, drawn to the energy and culture they saw in her clients' posts — they wanted to be part of something that looked genuinely fun, real, and effective. Her reputation hadn't just grown. It had elevated.

Her success came from many factors — but it didn't truly take off until the trust signals were there, so that strangers across her community could see she was the right choice for their specific fitness journey.

The mechanics are identical for your practice. When your reviews, testimonials, and client-generated content reflect the genuine quality of your care, you don't just attract more clients — you attract better-fit clients. The pet owner who values your exotic expertise and books immediately. The family that sees your team's warmth in a video and drives past two other clinics to get to you with both their dogs and a cat. The horse owner who heard about you in three different places before they ever called. Trust signals don't just fill your schedule. They fill it with the right people.

As a veterinarian, this strategy works powerfully in your favor. I'm not saying ads won't play a role — for a veterinary practice, a steady and consistent flow of new clients requires more than word-of-mouth alone. But trust signals are the foundation everything else is built on. Without them, even great ads will underperform.

What the Research Says

Today's pet owners rely on reviews more heavily than ever. Recent consumer behavior research from the Pew Research Center found that 82% of U.S. adults check online ratings or reviews at least sometimes before making a purchase for the first time — with 40% doing so almost always. People trust online reviews nearly as much as personal recommendations, and they typically read multiple reviews before deciding which business to call.

For veterinary care specifically, they're looking for three things: reassurance, compassion, and evidence of clinical competence. Your reviews are where they find all three.

Reputation as a Competitive Advantage

Your reviews are not simply compliments on your medical skill. They are strategic assets.

A clinic with 200 positive reviews earned over the past three years appears more established, more trusted, and more active than one with 90 reviews accumulated over a decade. Recency matters as much as volume — and both matter more than most practice owners realize.

Reviews directly affect:

- **Search ranking** — the more reviews you earn consistently, the more relevant you appear to Google and AI search tools
- **Client confidence** — people trust volume and recency over a single perfect score
- **Conversion rates** — high-star clinics win more phone calls and booking requests
- **Perceived expertise** — detailed, specific reviews shape expectations before the first visit
- **Pricing perception** — clinics with strong reputations experience less resistance to treatment estimates because clients already trust their integrity

Volume, Recency, and the Power of Staying Visible

A five-star rating is great — but it's not enough on its own.

Volume establishes credibility. Recency establishes relevance. When there is consistent, recent activity surrounding your clinic — Google updates, social posts, fresh reviews, new videos, new client testimonials — something important happens. It creates what's known as recency bias: the tendency for people to perceive the most recently active option as the most relevant and trustworthy one.

To understand how this plays out in a real veterinary setting, consider the experience of my client Dr. Ashley Tuma, who ran a clinic near Lancaster, Pennsylvania. For years, her practice thrived on word-of-mouth and the deep loyalty she had built within her rural community. Clients knew her, trusted her, and consistently referred their neighbors and friends. But like many veterinarians, Dr. Tuma had gone relatively quiet online. Her website was stable, her Facebook page was occasionally updated, and she didn't post much beyond the basics. Nothing was wrong — there was just nothing new.

Then we updated her strategy.

Dr. Tuma began sharing authentic video testimonials from real clients — short, heartfelt clips filmed right in her clinic, telling the stories of pets she had helped. She paired these with a steady rhythm of social media posts: patient highlights, educational tips, and behind-the-scenes moments that gave the community a window into the culture and compassion that defined her team.

Within weeks, she noticed a shift. New client numbers jumped almost immediately. But what surprised her even more was the surge in returning clients — people who already trusted her but hadn't been in for a while — who were saying things like, "I saw your video and realized I've been meaning to bring Daisy in," and "Your posts reminded me my cat is overdue for her exam."

This is recency bias at work. Even though Dr. Tuma had been an excellent veterinarian for years, what people were responding to wasn't her long history — it was the recent visibility of her care. The more active she became, the more the community perceived the clinic as engaged, modern, and growing.

The results were undeniable. Over the course of the following year, the numbers told a clear story. Impressions reached 1,518,642 — up 208%. Engagements climbed to 120,034 — up 79%. Post link clicks jumped 384.9%. Their audience grew by 65.1% to 2,602 followers, with 1,112 posts published — up 69.5% from the year before. And perhaps most telling of all, website visitors nearly tripled — growing from 5,614 in year one to 16,342 in year two.

More new appointments, more returning clients, and increased production and revenue followed. And best of all — she opened a second clinic, a brand-new building she designed herself, about ten miles away in Lancaster.

Nothing about her medical care had changed. What changed was taking a strategic approach to her marketing and building a solid foundation.

HOW TO EARN REVIEWS AUTHENTICALLY

You don't need gimmicks. You need moments.

I've spoken with many doctors who feel uncomfortable asking for reviews. If that hesitation resonates with you, let's address it directly — because this is something worth getting past. Google actually encourages businesses to ask for reviews. Their own Google Business Profile Help pages instruct practice owners to use their review link and share it with clients via email and text. Google wants you to collect reviews on their platform. You're not gaming the system — you're using it as intended.

The key is timing. The right moment to ask is when a client is relieved, grateful, or genuinely impressed — right after a successful visit, a warm conversation with a doctor, or a gentle treatment of a pet they were worried about. Train your team to recognize those moments and respond to them naturally.

Something as simple as this works beautifully: *"We're so glad we could help today. If you have a moment, leaving us a quick Google review really helps other pet owners in our community find good care — and honestly, our team loves reading them too."*

This works because it's true. Most clients understand what it takes to run a small business, and they genuinely want to support a practice they feel good about. Leaving a review validates their own decision to choose you. You're giving them an easy way to help.

A few additional tools to build your review engine:

- Place a QR code sign at checkout and in treatment rooms — linking directly to your Google review page
- Use your practice management software to send an automated follow-up text the next day — warm, not pushy
- Make review requests part of your team's regular workflow, not an afterthought

The key is honesty at the right moment, not pressure.

How to Respond to Reviews — Including the Negative Ones

Responding to reviews signals to both clients and search systems that you are active, engaged, and accountable. It's widely understood that Google's algorithms factor in review responses — including the keywords used in both reviews and replies — when ranking and recommending local businesses. Responding is not optional. It's part of your marketing.

Positive reviews deserve genuine gratitude. Negative reviews deserve professionalism and calm. A measured, thoughtful response to a critical review can actually increase trust — it demonstrates maturity, confidence, and a commitment to doing right by your clients.

A simple framework for negative reviews:

- Acknowledge the concern
- Stay calm and factual
- Keep your response brief
- Invite the client to continue the conversation privately

Never argue. Never reveal client details. Never let emotion guide your response. Keep the high ground — always. Everyone reading that exchange is a potential future client.

When a Review Crosses the Line

Not every negative review deserves only a response — some deserve a report.

Google has a built-in tool that allows business owners to flag reviews that violate their policies. This includes fake reviews, reviews left by someone who was never a client, reviews designed to deliberately damage your reputation, or reviews that contain false accusations. To access it, log into your Google Business Profile, navigate to the review in question, and click the three dots beside it. From there you can select "Report review" and follow Google's guidelines for the violation type.

I coached a client through this exact situation not long ago. A practice owner in Utah was targeted by a former disgruntled employee who created a fake Google account and used it to post a damaging, false review — full of accusations designed to tarnish the doctor's reputation. It was calculated and it was ugly. He was distraught and already on the phone with his attorney. I calmed him down, and here is what we did.

First, I had him respond to the review professionally and calmly — acknowledging that the experience described didn't align with the clinic's standards and inviting the reviewer to contact the practice directly. No emotion. No defensiveness. Pure professionalism. Then we reported the review through Google's reporting tool, documenting the policy violation clearly.

The review was removed.

The lesson here is important: you are not powerless in the face of a bad-faith attack on your reputation. Google's policies exist to protect legitimate businesses from fake and malicious reviews — but only if you know how to use the tools available to you. Respond professionally first. Report second. And never — under any circumstances — engage in a public argument with a reviewer, regardless of how unfair or false the review may be. The high ground is always the right ground.

"Research from Northwestern University's Spiegel Research Center found that a rating between 4.2 and 4.5 stars is generally considered more trustworthy than a perfect 5.0. A flawless score can raise suspicion of fake reviews — causing some prospective clients to hesitate. Don't be discouraged by the occasional imperfect review. In the right range, it actually helps."

Other Forms of Social Proof

Reviews are just one piece of the trust puzzle. Social proof also includes:

- **Video testimonials** — short, authentic clips from real clients carry enormous weight
- **Before-and-after cases** — shared through photos or video with client permission
- **Team spotlights** — shared on social media, in newsletters, or via email
- **User-generated content (UGC)** — when clients post about your practice on their own social profiles, it is one of the most powerful forms of promotion available today. It's third-party validation that no ad budget can replicate

TURN YOUR HAPPY CLIENTS INTO YOUR BEST MARKETERS

Here's something you can implement this week to start generating user-generated content immediately. Place a sign in your lobby that reads:

"Every client who posts about their pet on social media during their visit is entered into our monthly raffle for _________. Just tag our clinic and use #_________ to be entered!"

Make sure your entire team is talking this up with happy clients — especially anyone known to have a strong social following in your community. One enthusiastic client with 5,000 followers posting about their experience at your clinic is worth more than most paid campaigns. That's activating your community to support you.

Reputation Is Marketing You Can't Buy

You can purchase ads. You cannot purchase trust.

When you build your reputation as the foundation of your growth strategy, you win the long game. While most people think of this work as marketing, it is really public relations — and the return on investment is unlike anything else. A strong reputation attracts higher-quality clients, reduces your marketing costs, improves conversion rates, and enhances team morale.

And there's one more benefit worth mentioning: young associate veterinarians want to work for practices that are successful, respected, and culturally vibrant. A strong online reputation doesn't just attract clients — it attracts the talented staff who will help you serve them.

PRACTICE STEP: BUILD YOUR REVIEW ENGINE IN ONE AFTERNOON

Here's a simple, three-part action you can execute this week.

1. Add a QR Code at Checkout: Print a few QR code review signs — or ask your marketing agency to create them. The QR code should link directly to your Google review page. Place signs in your treatment rooms and at the front desk. Over the next few days, personally ask five happy clients to scan it on their way out. Watch what happens.

2. Create a Review Request Script for Your Team: Keep it simple and warm: "If you enjoyed your visit today, leaving us a quick Google review really helps other pet owners find good care."

✓ *At your next staff meeting or weekly huddle, teach every team member to use it naturally. Role-play it. Make it feel comfortable and genuine — because it is.*

3. Send a Follow-Up Message: Set up an automated email or text through your practice management system — sent the day after the visit — that reads something like: *"Thank you for trusting us with [pet name]. If you'd like to share your experience, here's a link to leave us a review: [link]."*

Simple. Warm. Effective.

Within one week, you'll see results. Within one month, you'll have momentum. Within one year, you'll have the strongest reputation in your market.

In the next chapter, we'll look at social media and community presence — how to show up consistently where your clients already are, build relationships before they ever need an appointment, and turn your online following into a steady stream of loyal, long-term clients.

Chapter Six

SOCIAL MEDIA: THE TRUST ACCELERATOR

"If you share good stuff, people will reshare it, and you will get more interaction and more followers."

— Guy Kawasaki, Bestselling Author and Speaker;
Early Apple Evangelist

The quote, while simple, captures an essential truth.

Social media is not about chasing trends, posting every day, or turning your veterinary practice into an entertainment brand. For a veterinary practice, social media serves a far more important purpose: building trust before a client ever walks through your door.

In the first chapter of this book, I laid out the marketing system we're building — step by step, in the correct order.

You learned that everything begins with Message–Market Fit: having absolute clarity about who your practice serves and how you serve them differently and meaningfully. Without that clarity, no website, ad campaign, or social channel can perform consistently.

From there, we moved into Findability — making sure your practice appears where pet owners are already looking. Today that means more than just Google. Pet owners are increasingly turning to AI tools like ChatGPT, Google Gemini, and Perplexity to ask questions like *"What's the best veterinary clinic near me for exotic pets?"* or *"Who's the most trusted vet in [city] for senior dog care?"* A strong local search presence, an accurate Google Business Profile, consistent information across the web, and a humanized website ensure that when someone searches — whether on Google or through an AI tool — they can find you quickly and feel confident they're in the right place.

You also saw how trust compounds through reviews, real imagery, and clear service pages that demonstrate real care, real people, and real expertise.

At this point in the system, something important has happened:

- Your **message** is clear.
- Your **foundation** is visible.
- Your practice is **discoverable.**

But there is still a gap between being findable and being chosen.

That gap is exactly where social media fits.

Social media is not a replacement for search, a shortcut to growth, or a substitute for paid advertising. Instead, it functions as your practice's trust accelerator — a way for prospective clients to observe your practice long before they ever need you urgently.

For many pet owners, social media is where they:

- **Quietly evaluate** you over time
- **Learn** how you think about care
- **Decide** whether you feel safe, modern, and compassionate
- **Confirm** that real people stand behind your practice

The Social Check

Just last week, I was at a video shoot with a client outside Raleigh, North Carolina. A patient was sitting in front of me, recording a testimonial for the website and YouTube. She mentioned how a friend had recommended the practice, then added — almost offhandedly — *"So I scrolled through his social media accounts immediately. I could tell he was a real person, with real patients who genuinely trusted him. And I could tell the office was nice."*

I asked her to clarify what she meant about checking social media first.

She laughed and said, *"Oh yeah — I'm a millennial. I'd never do business with someone without checking their socials first. I need to know they're legit, have real staff, and real patients talking about good experiences. That's where I confirm they're okay. Honestly, for me, social is even more important than reviews."*

She didn't just describe a habit. She described exactly how trust gets built — or lost — before an appointment is made.

In other words, social media answers a question Google search alone cannot: *"Do I feel comfortable trusting these people with my family — with my animal?"*

This matters deeply because later in the system — when we introduce Demand Capture tools like Google Ads and Meta advertising — those ads perform far better when familiarity and trust already exist. Paid traffic simply converts more efficiently when your practice doesn't feel unknown.

Social media creates the context for everything that follows.

Pet Owners Are Emotional Decision-Makers

Pet owners are protective, anxious, hopeful, and deeply attached to the animals they love. When they choose a veterinarian, they aren't just selecting a service — they're choosing a partner in the care of a family member. Social media allows that relationship to begin early, long before the moment of need.

And it may surprise you who is actually on social — and how often.

Yes, the averages say people spend roughly **two and a half hours per day on social media.** But the more important truth is this: social media is a dominant daily habit across nearly every generation of pet owners you serve. More than 80% of U.S. adults use at least one social platform. YouTube and Facebook remain the most widely used overall, followed closely by Instagram, while TikTok continues to grow among younger adults and families entering their prime pet-owning years.

When used intentionally, social media becomes an extension of your waiting room, your exam room, and your bedside manner. The question is not whether you should show up — but how to do it in a way that builds trust instead of noise.

THE ROLE OF SOCIAL MEDIA

One of the biggest mistakes practices make is treating social media as a stand-alone task instead of what it truly is: a supporting pillar inside a larger system.

Social media is not meant to replace search. It's not meant to replace referrals. And it's definitely not meant to replace paid advertising. Its role is far more subtle — and far more powerful.

Social media prepares demand.

Think of it this way: Google search and AI tools like ChatGPT capture people who are ready right now. Ads capture people in the moment of intent. Social media builds familiarity with people who are almost ready — or who will be ready later. It allows people to understand who you are without pressure. And that is exactly why it belongs before paid advertising in this system — not after it.

What Veterinary Social Media Is — And What It's Not

Let's reset expectations. Veterinary social media is not:

- **Posting every single day**
- **Chasing viral content**
- **Entertaining strangers who will never become clients**

Instead, veterinary social media is about familiarity. When someone sees your post and subconsciously thinks, "Oh, it's them again," you're doing it right.

I often tell clinics this: social media isn't about what you want to say — it's about what your future clients need to see repeatedly to feel safe.

It gives people repeated, low-pressure exposure to how your practice thinks, speaks, and behaves. Over time, that exposure removes uncertainty. It gives you a place to explain things calmly, show how decisions are made, demonstrate care without urgency, and let pet owners observe you before they have to trust you during a stressful moment.

Social Content to Focus On

The most effective social media content comes from the natural rhythm of your day.

It comes from conversations already happening in exam rooms, at the front desk, and in follow-up calls. It comes from the explanations you repeat multiple times a week, the reassurances you offer instinctively, and the moments when you see relief wash over a client's face because something finally makes sense.

That's the content.

Trust-building social media doesn't announce how good you are. It shows how you think. It lets people observe your approach to care before they ever experience it firsthand.

A short post explaining why you sometimes recommend monitoring instead of immediate intervention can do more to establish confidence than a dozen polished promotional graphics. A photo of a technician gently handling an anxious animal, paired with a calm explanation of your low-stress handling philosophy, communicates far more than any stock image ever could.

Here's something worth understanding about what performs best: posts featuring real humans — photos or videos, especially people experiencing genuine emotion — consistently outperform stock images and pet-only photos. People relate to people. They connect with joy, relief, laughter, and care. Think of it as emotional synchronicity — when viewers see someone feeling something real, they feel it too. And that connection is what makes them remember you.

In a marketing workshop I delivered in February 2026, I talked about how emotional connection drives engagement far more effectively than information alone. Nobody gets excited about a Canva graphic that reads "3 Reasons to Brush Your Dog's Teeth" over a stock photo. But a short video of a certified veterinary technician actually brushing a dog's teeth while explaining the technique? That's useful, a little entertaining, and genuinely shareable.

Two recent examples that bear this out: a candid group photo of a team at a shelter event generated huge engagement. A few teammates celebrating a Friday donut reward sparked dozens of community congratulations. What do both have in common? They told the audience something important without saying a word: *this is a healthy, fun, caring team — and I would trust them with my pet.*

One practice we worked with began sharing simple "Here's what we commonly see" explanations — nothing dramatic, nothing clinical. Just doctors and techs talking clearly, without jargon, about real situations clients worry about all the time. Within a few months, new clients began referencing those posts during appointments. They weren't quoting facts — they were referencing comfort. They came in feeling prepared instead of defensive.

That's the real outcome you're aiming for.

A Word on Using AI for Social Media

AI tools like ChatGPT or Claude can be genuinely useful in your social media workflow — but it's worth being clear about where they help and where they don't.

AI is excellent for generating caption ideas, drafting post copy, suggesting hashtags, brainstorming content themes for the month ahead, writing scripts for short videos, and helping you find the right words when you know what you want to say but can't quite say it. It can also help you identify trending topics in veterinary care that your community might be interested in — giving you a starting point rather than a blank page.

What AI cannot — and should not — replace is the real content itself. The actual photo of your technician calming an anxious cat. The genuine video of your team celebrating a patient's recovery. The authentic testimonial from a client whose dog you saved. These moments are irreplaceable precisely because they are human and real — and your audience knows the difference.

AI-generated images and videos of fake staff, fake patients, or fabricated clinic scenes have no place in a trust-building social strategy. Pet owners are perceptive. Anything that feels manufactured or inauthentic will quietly undermine the very confidence you're working to build.

Use AI to find your words and spark your ideas. Use your phone and your real team to capture the moments. That combination — human content guided by smart tools — is where the magic lives.

CONTENT IDEAS TO GET YOU STARTED

Here are practical content ideas drawn directly from the natural rhythm of a veterinary practice:

- Videos of you or your team performing a treatment or procedure
- Staff spotlights — highlight a team member each week
- A short video introducing a new blog post on your website, ending with "check it out on our website!"
- Contests or giveaways that spark user-generated content — "share this" or "tag us" to enter
- Before-and-after photos or stories with client permission
- Client success stories paired with real photos or video
- Video testimonials from happy clients
- Behind-the-scenes moments from your clinic culture
- Photos with clients and their pets
- Upcoming event announcements
- Team outings, awards, or celebrations
- Treats or meals for the staff — show the team's genuine reaction
- Gifts received from grateful clients — photo of the doctor or team responding authentically
- Holiday posts and fun seasonal content — costumes encouraged

Keep this list handy and refer to it when you're not sure what to post next. The answer is almost always right in front of you.

Choosing the Right Platforms

You don't need to master every platform. Trying to do so usually dilutes your effort and burns out whoever is managing it.

For most veterinary practices, **Facebook and Instagram** remain the most practical places to begin. These platforms are where a wide range of pet owners already spend time, and they naturally support the kinds of content that build trust: photos, short videos, explanations, and stories.

YouTube serves a different role. It's not a feed — it's a library. YouTube becomes a place where people can hear your tone and observe how you explain things when no one is rushing you. A handful of thoughtful videos, even simple ones, can quietly work for you for years. Client testimonials especially thrive on YouTube. While YouTube Shorts exist, they're generally less valuable than your regular posting rhythm on Facebook and Instagram — use them as a bonus, not a primary strategy.

TikTok may or may not fit your practice — and that's perfectly okay. If you have a young team member who loves creating TikToks and wants to run with it, let them. But if a platform feels forced, uncomfortable, or unsustainable, it's rarely the right place to build lasting trust.

Social media should feel like a natural extension of how you already communicate. Start where it feels most natural and build from there.

Posting Frequency, Consistency, and Real Life

Don't burn out. Quality over quantity — always.

Two or three meaningful posts per week are more than enough to keep your practice present and relevant in your community. That rhythm allows you to show up consistently without turning social media into a burden.

What matters most is that your presence doesn't disappear for weeks at a time — and that it is never replaced by stock photos or generic graphics. Silence creates uncertainty. Inconsistency creates doubt. But steady, imperfect participation builds confidence over time.

I've seen practices gain more traction from a fun photo with a puppy and a couple of phone-shot videos per week — unpolished, real, honest — than from beautifully produced content that's impossible to sustain. Done is better than perfect. Consistent is better than impressive.

HOW SOCIAL MEDIA MAKES YOUR ADS WORK BETTER

This is where your marketing system connects most powerfully.

When someone clicks a Google ad for your practice, they rarely stop at the landing page. They look around. They scan. They search your name. And often, they check your social media — just like the millennial patient I described earlier in this chapter.

What they find there either reinforces confidence or reintroduces hesitation.

A living, human social feed reduces resistance. It confirms legitimacy. It answers the emotional questions that ads and websites can't fully address on their own. Practices with strong, consistent social media presence often experience smoother ad performance — not because social media converts directly, but because it reduces doubt. People who already feel familiar with your practice require less convincing. They book more readily. They compare you to competitors less aggressively. They trust your recommendations more quickly.

Ads create urgency. Social media creates confidence.

When both are aligned, you get something every practice owner wants: steady, sustainable, compounding growth.

In the next chapter, we'll shift into digital advertising on Google and Meta — focusing on capturing intent, targeting demand that already exists, and turning visibility into booked appointments. But keep this in mind as we move forward: the social foundation you build today is what makes every ad dollar you spend tomorrow work harder.

Scan for free access to social media scripts for veterinary reels and shorts.

Chapter Seven

DIGITAL ADVERTISING

"Many a small thing has been made large by the right kind of advertising."

– Mark Twain

Why Ads Come Last —Not First

Many practices want to start here — but shouldn't. The common refrain is: *"I need new clients now!"* or *"Can we just run ads to drive new clients first, and then clean up the website and social media later once we have the revenue?"*

I went through this exact situation with a client from the midwestern U.S. not long ago. I knew their campaign had very little chance of success — their website was broken, their social media was thin, and their messaging was unclear across several specialty services. But they wanted to try anyway.

Their request was straightforward: *"Let's just run the ads. Once they bring in more money, we'll clean everything else up."*

Let me walk you through what we found when we looked at their website. First, it loaded slowly. When someone clicks an ad and gets a spinning loading wheel, credibility drops immediately — the unspoken question becomes: *why can't they afford a proper website?* Their video banner was pulling from YouTube and displaying YouTube interface elements, which looked awkward and unprofessional. Scroll further down the page, and the same video appeared again as an "About Us" feature — as if no one had noticed it was identical to the hero banner. Scroll a little further and there was a link to "Listen to the Doctor's Podcast" — except it was a single interview from two years ago, nearly impossible to actually play.

The copy throughout the site was vague, with remnants of old keyword-stuffing attempts that read unnaturally to human visitors — and worse, sent confusing signals to AI tools like ChatGPT that were looking for clear, specific answers about services and expertise.

Their social media wasn't any stronger. It consisted mostly of generic Canva graphics — stock quotes, templated health tips, and recycled national awareness posts. Almost no real people. No real moments.

My recommendation was clear: get the foundation right first. When ads run, they place a microscope on your business. If things are a mess underneath, the ads simply make that mess visible to more people. The results aren't just poor — they can be actively damaging to your reputation.

I should have held my ground. Instead, I agreed to move forward. The traffic came in — but the results didn't. Clicks didn't convert into appointments. Leads hesitated. Cost per lead crept upward. People visited the site and left. After six months, they concluded that we simply weren't good at Google Ads and canceled their contract.

The truth was different. The ads did exactly what they were supposed to do: they brought attention. What failed was everything waiting on the other side of that attention. The website didn't answer questions clearly. The messaging didn't reduce uncertainty. The social presence didn't reinforce trust.

Advertising amplified what already existed — and what already existed wasn't ready.

That experience changed how I work with clients. I now hold the line on sequence — not to be difficult, but because I've seen firsthand what happens when we don't. A good agency should tell you the truth, even when it's not what you want to hear. That's what I committed to doing from that point forward.

This is what happens when you start in the middle of the system. Advertising is not a rescue tool. It doesn't fix broken foundations. It doesn't compensate for unclear messaging. And it doesn't create trust where none has been built.

That's why this book insists on sequence.

Digital advertising is an accelerator — and accelerators only work when the foundation underneath them is solid.

WHEN ADVERTISING IS THE RIGHT NEXT STEP

There comes a point in your growth where good awareness and word-of-mouth are no longer enough on their own. You've built a strong foundation. Your brand, culture, and reputation are in place. Now you need fuel to take your practice to the next level — maybe you've added an associate, expanded your facilities, or simply want to grow beyond the ceiling that organic growth alone creates.

I've spoken with many independent veterinary practice owners who avoided digital ads under the assumption that they were too expensive, too complicated, or unnecessary for a clinic built on long-standing loyalty. Meanwhile, a new breed of corporate competitors moved in — pouring millions into online advertising and quietly reshaping how pet owners make choices. They bought the first impression. The top slot. The immediate visibility that today's search-driven culture rewards.

And the truth is simple: in almost every community, corporate chains aren't growing because they provide better medicine — far from it. They are growing because they show up first and have made choosing them the easy option, often capturing less discerning pet owners in moments of urgency.

When ads are done well, they allow your clinic to highlight its strengths, promote specific services, and attract high-intent pet owners exactly when demand peaks. Ads can fill slow days, promote seasonal services, launch new programs, introduce new doctors, and strategically grow the areas of your practice that deserve more attention.

And unlike traditional advertising — print mailers, billboards, sponsorships — digital ads cost significantly less and are far easier to measure. You can see what's working, adjust quickly, and guide your investment with clarity rather than hope.

But not all ads are created equal.

There is a meaningful difference between boosting a post and running a well-structured campaign. There is a difference between appearing in someone's newsfeed and showing up the moment a pet owner types "vet near me" at 7:30 p.m. because their dog is suddenly limping.

In this chapter we're going to focus on the latter — the kind of digital advertising that actually works for veterinary practices. The kind that attracts new clients without wasting your money. And even if you plan to hand this work to an agency, I want to give you enough understanding to oversee it confidently, ask the right questions, and hold the right standards.

The Three Roles of Digital Advertising

Think of digital ads as serving 3 distinct but complementary roles:

- **Intent Capture** — meeting high-intent searches ("vet near me," "emergency vet," "dog dental cleaning") the moment they occur
- **Demand Creation** — introducing your services and value to pet owners who weren't actively searching but are open to better care
- **Demand Recapture** — reminding recent website visitors, social media engagers, and video viewers to take the next step

What we want to accomplish for your practice is to get these three working together — so that your flow of new clients becomes predictable, steady, and increasingly efficient over time.

Google Search Ads — Intent-Based Advertising

Google Search Ads remain the most powerful and most direct form of digital advertising available to a veterinary practice. These ads meet pet owners at the height of their intention. When someone types "veterinarian near me," "emergency vet," or "dog dental cleaning," they're not casually browsing — they're looking for help, making a decision, and ready to act.

This is why Google Search is often called "high-intent advertising." It doesn't try to create demand. It captures demand that already exists.

At its core, Google Ads work by matching what a pet owner types — "cat vomiting St. Petersburg," for example — with ads from clinics that can help. The clinic willing to bid more will often appear higher, but relevance and quality matter just as much. You don't need to outspend corporate competitors. You need to out-match them. And that starts with choosing the right keywords.

Think of keywords as the doorways through which new clients enter your practice. Some are broad and local:

- "Veterinarian near me"
- "Animal hospital [your city]"
- "Emergency vet"
- "[Species] vet [your city]"

Others are service-specific:

- "Dog dental cleaning"
- "Spay and neuter cost"

- “Cat X-ray”
- “Rabbit vet”
- “Laser therapy for dogs”

And then there are urgency-driven searches — “same-day vet appointment” or “open now” — which are incredibly effective for practices offering sick-pet availability.

The smartest way to structure campaigns is by intent. Group emergency terms together, dental terms together, exotic pet terms together. Each group reflects a different mindset and urgency level. This avoids wasted spend and ensures that the message a pet owner sees matches exactly what they searched for.

Geographic targeting matters just as much. Many clinics try to reach everyone within a wide radius — but broader doesn’t mean better. A tight geographic area, either by ZIP code or a realistic radius around your clinic, improves relevance and reduces cost. You want to reach the pet owners who can actually make it to your practice.

Google also rewards clarity. Adding your clinic’s phone number, address, hours, and other details — known as ad extensions — makes your ad more trustworthy and immediately actionable. Sync your business hours so ads don’t run after you’re closed, unless you intentionally support after-hours calls. And treat phone calls as the conversions that matter most. A call is not a “maybe” — a call is a real opportunity. Track them. Review them. Improve them.

Every Google campaign must lead to a destination page that matches the ad. A pet owner searching for dental care should land on your dental page — not your homepage. Someone searching “emergency vet” should immediately see your triage message, hours, and phone number. The tighter the match between ad and landing page, the higher the conversion rate.

This is where Google Ads become truly powerful: they allow your practice to win the "I need a vet now" moment — the decisive instant when a pet owner stops searching and starts choosing. If you're present in that moment, you win new clients. If you're not, someone else will.

Meta Ads — Capturing Attention on Facebook and Instagram

If Google Search Ads capture intention, Meta Ads — on Facebook and Instagram — capture attention. While Google thrives on answering urgent questions, Meta thrives on human connection. It's where people go to check in, scroll, and feel part of something familiar.

Research from Kantar, a leading global data and analytics company, consistently shows that Meta platforms are among the most efficient brand-building environments available — driving emotional connection and positive brand sentiment at scale. Independent ad strategists echo the same finding: Meta isn't just an ad platform. It's a reputation engine.

This makes Meta uniquely valuable for veterinary practices. Pet owners may not log into Facebook or Instagram looking for a veterinarian — but they are looking for stories, emotion, and animal moments they can relate to. When they encounter your practice in that environment, they aren't evaluating a transaction. They're evaluating you.

Meta ads are at their best when your practice feels genuinely human — when pet owners see your team in real moments: comforting a nervous patient, celebrating a successful procedure, welcoming a new doctor, or simply being themselves. This authentic, human quality is what separates Meta advertising from every other channel. And when you run paid ads on top of an already strong organic social presence, the results can be extraordinary.

A Real-World Example: Advanced Pet Care Clinic

Advanced Pet Care Clinic in Iowa, owned by Dr. Tammy, has been a Walker Kreative client for many years. When we first partnered, the clinic averaged around forty new clients per month and had struggled to break past that ceiling. In one of our early conversations, Dr. Tammy shared her goal: she'd love to reach fifty new clients per month consistently. That single shift, she told me, would reduce stress across the entire practice.

Before any paid campaigns were launched, the foundation was already strong. Through their own efforts and their work with Walker Kreative, they had established clear messaging, well-defined branding, a positive community reputation, strong reviews, and professional video assets featured on their website and a new YouTube channel. The trust, credibility, and goodwill were built and continuously being worked on. What they lacked was a consistent and scalable source of new attention.

It's worth noting: a practice could look at all that foundational work and feel like nothing has happened yet. In reality, it was exactly the preparation needed for the next stage. The ads had a solid platform to land on.

We implemented a paid campaign with Meta Ads as the primary engine, supplemented by Google Search Ads to capture high-intent traffic. Once activated, the results came quickly. The clinic surpassed its goal of fifty almost immediately — then kept climbing. They recorded sixty-five new clients, then sixty-seven, sixty-six, sixty-three, and reached a peak of seventy in a single month. These were not isolated spikes. They were a sustained shift, week after week.

Over six weeks of our analysis, the clinic gained roughly eighty new clients above their long-standing average. At the industry benchmark of approximately $600 in annual revenue per client, those eighty additional clients represent nearly $50,000 in new annual revenue. Projected over multiple years — even accounting for normal attrition — those same eighty clients can generate more than $100,000 in cumulative revenue. The total ad spend for the entire year was approximately $15,000. That's an extraordinary return on ad spend.

And this doesn't account for multi-pet households, higher-value procedures, emergency care, or referrals — all of which meaningfully expand the real lifetime value.

The advertising didn't create something from nothing. It amplified a foundation that was already strong. The clinic's messaging, branding, reviews, and professional presence made the advertising more effective. Paid traffic didn't replace their organic strengths — it unlocked them.

What Meta Ads Work Best For

There are three major categories where Facebook and Instagram ads consistently shine for veterinary practices:

Service promotions — Dental month, puppy and kitten packages, senior wellness visits, laser therapy for chronic pain. These are services where a clear message paired with a compelling visual or short video can nudge a pet owner to take action.

Clinic storytelling — Behind-the-scenes moments, staff spotlights, patient success stories with permission, and everyday glimpses of life inside your practice. These ads build trust before the client ever walks through your door.

Local awareness — Simple, powerful messages like "Now accepting new patients," "Meet our new doctor," or "Same-day sick pet appointments available." These campaigns quietly remind your community that you are here, you are active, and you are ready to help.

Getting Started with Meta Ads

Whether you're setting up ads yourself or simply want to understand what your agency should be doing for you, here are the essentials.

Use a tight geographic radius — your true service area — combined with basic age filters and, where available, pet-owner interest categories. Keep in mind that Meta's algorithm is highly sophisticated. Over-targeting actually reduces performance. Let your message and storytelling do the filtering.

Whenever possible, use video. Not glossy, over-produced video — authentic, sincere video. A doctor speaking for twenty seconds in a quiet exam room will outperform a polished agency commercial because it feels real. Based on our experience running campaigns for clients over many years, Meta's algorithms also appear to favor authentic-feeling video content over heavily produced material.

When someone clicks your ad, send them to a specific landing page with one clear purpose: call, book, or fill out a short form. If the ad is about dental cleanings, the landing page should be about dental cleanings. Specificity builds confidence and ensures your ads convert.

YouTube Advertising

YouTube is one of my favorite platforms — and for good reason. Video is a powerful communicator. Every client where we've had the opportunity to shoot a great set of videos, create compelling ads, and establish a solid YouTube channel has experienced stable, compounding growth.

Google Search Ads capture consumers when they're actively searching. Meta connects with consumers emotionally. YouTube establishes a deeper level of understanding. This is the platform where pet owners go to learn, watch, and have things explained clearly. And in veterinary medicine — where fear, confusion, and uncertainty often drive behavior — clarity is a genuine competitive advantage.

Short, sincere videos can move mountains. A thirty-second to one-minute video titled "What to Expect at Your Puppy's First Exam" or "How We Care for Anxious Cats" builds trust instantly. A doctor explaining "Why Dental Cleanings Matter More Than You Think" or "What Lameness Looks Like in Horses" demonstrates expertise in a way that a text article with a stock photo never could.

These videos don't need studio lighting or a film crew. Even when we produce professional video for our clients at Walker Kreative, we pay close attention to producing content the way pet owners want to consume it — which is not overly polished. Authenticity is vital. A veterinarian speaking warmly from an exam room feels relatable. A technician demonstrating how they calm a nervous pet feels reassuring. A doctor walking through a dental procedure with before-and-after photos feels credible and real.

YouTube ads allow you to take this educational content and show it directly to pet owners in your community. When set up as skippable in-stream ads — targeted by geography, species interest, or even recent Google search behavior — they become powerful tools for shaping perception and positioning your practice as a trusted authority.

YouTube ads are not about going viral. They are about reassurance:

- *"This clinic knows what they're doing."*
- *"These are real professionals."*
- *"I trust them."*
- *"I feel good about choosing this place."*

This doesn't always result in a booking the same day — and I've had many conversations with practice owners about when the numbers will move. But YouTube advertising creates a powerful bond that influences every future decision. When a pet owner finally needs dental work, surgery, exotic care, or urgent help, they won't have to search. They'll remember the doctor who taught them something valuable. The clinic that felt calm, confident, and competent. The practice that felt human.

That is the real power of YouTube advertising.

Retargeting: Your Second Chance to Win the Client

Not every pet owner books on the first click — in fact, most don't. They see an ad, visit your website, watch a video, or browse your services, and then life intervenes. A child calls. A meeting starts. The urgency fades. And even though they were interested, they move on.

Back in the golden age of Madison Avenue, marketers believed it took seven "touches" before someone took action after seeing an ad. Today, with the volume of media surrounding us at every moment, that number is far higher. This is where retargeting becomes a valuable tool in your digital advertising strategy.

Retargeting automatically and consistently follows up with people who have already shown interest in your clinic — reminding them to schedule or call. These are not cold prospects. They are warm leads who already know your name, have seen your message, and have considered you. Retargeting reaches three types of pet owners:

Website visitors — People who have already browsed your services, read about your team, or looked at your hours. They were close. Sometimes just one click away.

Social engagers — Anyone who has liked, commented, shared, or watched your videos on Facebook, Instagram, or YouTube has shown genuine emotional interest. They're paying attention.

High-intent searchers — Through certain ad setups, you can retarget people whose recent search behavior shows they're actively exploring veterinary care — even if they never visited your site directly.

Consider the pet owner who clicked your Facebook ad for dental cleanings with mild interest — their dog has bad breath — but then got distracted. Later that evening, they see a follow-up ad: *"Considering a dental cleaning for your pet? Our gentle, same-day procedures help prevent pain and keep your pet healthy. Book your dental evaluation today."* That's retargeting at work.

Or consider a client who visits your puppy care page but doesn't book. The next morning on Instagram they see a video of you speaking authentically about new puppy vaccines and early care. They click "Learn More," land back on the puppy care page, and call your office.

Retargeting functions like a quiet, helpful reminder — not a pushy pitch. It says: *"We see you. We're here when you're ready."*

Retargeting is handled on each specific platform. In other words, you manage this on Meta Ads Manager for Facebook and Instagram, Google Ads Manager for Google and YouTube. Once in place, it automatically shows your ads to anyone who visited a web page, watched a video on YouTube, or engaged with your social content.

Retargeting is the bridge between awareness and action — the invisible assistant working behind the scenes, keeping your clinic top of mind until the pet owner is ready to choose you.

What Not to Do — So You Don't Burn Your Budget

Digital advertising is powerful, but it's also one of the fastest ways to waste money when used incorrectly. Many clinics that have claimed "ads don't work" weren't failing at advertising — they were failing at strategy.

Here are the four most common mistakes I've seen repeatedly:

Mistake 1 — Boosting random posts and calling it a strategy. Boosting can occasionally help with visibility or engagement, but it is not the same as running an intentional campaign. A boosted post has no targeting structure, conversion tracking, or strategic purpose. It's like putting a flyer on 100 telephone poles and hoping someone who needs a veterinarian happens to walk past. Not a terrible thing to do, but its a shot in the metaphorical dark.

Mistake 2 — Sending ad clicks to a generic homepage. Your homepage is designed to inform — not to convert for a specific service. When someone clicks an ad for laser therapy or acupuncture and lands on a general website, they encounter friction. They start scanning, looking for the right tab, trying to decode options. As confusion rises, motivation falls. Every click needs a clear, matched destination.

Mistake 3 — Over-targeting or under-targeting. Some clinics target too narrowly — specific age, income, interest, behavior, location, and device — which drives costs up and reduces results. Others target too broadly, wasting impressions on people who don't own pets or live too far away. The most effective strategy is straightforward: a realistic radius and a message that does the filtering. The algorithms behind Google and Meta today are sophisticated and do much of the heavy lifting.

Mistake 4 — Slow or no follow-up. This is the one I see most often — and it quietly destroys more ad campaigns than any other factor. Ads create opportunities, not appointments. If your team doesn't answer the phone promptly, respond to web forms quickly, or return missed calls the same day, your return on ad spend collapses. Do you have a webchat that is AI enhanced to handle after-hours visitors? This type of tool can answer urgent questions and get contact information for the next day. Never launch an ad campaign without first confirming that your lead handling systems are going to work.

I've seen practices run ads for puppy visits, generate five legitimate leads through a web form, and then let those leads sit unanswered in an email inbox for a week because "we're too busy to check emails." Those five leads represented real families — and real revenue — lost forever to a competitor.

I also recently worked with a practice that changed phone system providers. Their new client phone number had changed — but no one noticed the old number was still on the website. The clinic was generating calls that were never arriving at the front desk. Lost leads they were paying for. And even worse, those leads were reaching a number that didn't work — permanently destroying their confidence in that business.

Test every step of your campaign before launching. Make sure every lead can reach you, and that someone is ready to respond fast.

MAKING GOOD ADS

Some services have a natural marketing advantage because they are emotionally compelling, time-sensitive, or tied to clear outcomes. Here are the categories we've found most effective:

Dental Cleanings — Clients can see the impact. The health benefits are well established, the visuals are powerful, and urgency peaks during February's Dental Health Month. But why limit it to February? A second promotional push in September can perform just as well and is rarely something your competitors are doing.

Puppy and Kitten Packages — These campaigns capture families during a joyful, high-commitment moment. New pet owners want guidance, and these packages open the door to years of loyalty.

Senior Pet Wellness — Mobility issues, pain management, and aging concerns resonate deeply. Senior pet owners are highly motivated and emotionally invested in improving their animal's quality of life.

Laser Therapy for Rehabilitation — Before-and-after content is especially effective here. Senior pets are the primary audience, but rehabilitation cases offer a more niche and highly targeted opportunity.

Exotic Pet Care — Few clinics offer this, which makes advertising remarkably efficient. When someone searches "rabbit vet" or "bearded dragon doctor," they're ready to book. You simply need to show up.

Same-Day or Urgent Appointments — When a pet is sick, hesitation disappears. These ads convert quickly and reliably because they meet an immediate need. If you offer urgent care, market it.

Each of these categories works best with one clear service per campaign, driving traffic to a specific, aligned landing page. This is how you maximize results and minimize wasted spend.

CREATING AN AD THAT CONVERTS

Every effective ad accomplishes three things: it names the situation, reduces anxiety, and invites action. A reliable structure looks like this:

1. **Problem**: Name what the client is experiencing. "Same-day sick pet appointments available."
2. **Reassurance**: Show proof with a real photo or video — never stock imagery — that their pet will be in good hands. A doctor's photo with a patient, or a calm client testimonial video, works beautifully here.
3. **What to Expect**: Set clear expectations. "You'll receive a full exam, clear recommendations, and a follow-up call."
4. **Call to Action**: Invite them to act. "Call now to schedule your visit."

Here's an example of ad copy that works — because it names the problem, provides reassurance, and delivers a clear call to action:

"Bad breath isn't just a smell — it's often a sign of dental disease. Our gentle cleanings help prevent pain, infection, and tooth loss. You'll get a clear exam, before-and-after photos, and a check-in call the next day. Call to schedule your pet's dental evaluation."

And remember: authenticity always outperforms polish. A simple thirty-second doctor video filmed in a well-lit room with clean audio will outperform a stock image every time. What clients want is honesty and humanity — not perfection.

The Landing Page

When someone clicks your ad, they need to arrive at a specific page on your website — not your homepage. We call this a landing page because they are landing on the exact page most relevant to the ad they clicked.

A strong landing page includes:

- A headline that matches or closely aligns with the ad
- Friendly, benefit-driven language — no jargon
- A simple "what to expect" section
- Trust signals — reviews, testimonials, doctor video, or real photos of your team doing the work described on that page
- One single, clear action: Schedule Now or Call Us Now

If your ad is about laser therapy, the landing page cannot be your general services list. Make the path obvious. Remove friction. Guide the pet owner confidently toward the next step. Every unnecessary click loses people. Every clear step keeps them.

How to Think About the Money

This is the conversation I have more than any other with practice owners. When your credit card is being charged by Google or Meta month after month, and you can't clearly see dollars translating into new appointments, it feels mysterious — even wasteful. You wonder: are people actually coming from the ads, or is it just the word-of-mouth you already had?

Here's how to think about it clearly:

Ads are not an expense. They are an investment.

THE TWO NUMBERS THAT DRIVE EVERY AD DECISION

CAC (Cost to Acquire a Client): How much you spend in advertising to gain one new client.

Target: keep your CAC at or below one-third of your client's first-year value.

LTV (LifeTime Value): How much revenue a typical new client generates over time — usually measured over the first one to two years.

Industry benchmark: approximately $600 per client in year one.

The Formula

Goal: 20 new clients per month Acceptable CAC: $150 Required monthly budget:

20 × $150 = $3,000 per month

This is not guesswork. This is math.

The 3:1 Rule: If a new client is worth $600 in their first year, spending $150–$200 to acquire them is a sound investment. Aim for at least three dollars returned for every dollar spent.

Where clinics get into trouble is with vague goals. Advertising must be grounded in numbers:

- How many new clients per month do you want?
- What is an acceptable CAC?
- What budget does that require?

UNDERSTANDING ROAS

ROAS — Return On Ad Spend — measures revenue divided by ad cost. It's an incredibly useful metric for service-specific campaigns.

If you spend $800 on a dental ad campaign in a month and it generates $4,000 in dental procedures, your ROAS is:

$4,000 ÷ $800 = 5× ROAS

For every dollar spent, you earned five.

WHAT DOES YOUR AD SPEND ACTUALLY RETURN?

THREE REAL EXAMPLES

Example 1 — Dental Month Campaign Ad spend: $1,000 Procedures booked: 8 Revenue per procedure: $600 Total revenue: $4,800

ROAS: 4.8× — for every $1 spent, you earned $4.80

Example 2 — Puppy Package Campaign Ad spend: $1,200 New puppies: 12 First-year value per puppy: $700 Total revenue: $8,400 **ROAS: 7× — for every $1 spent, you earned $7.00**

Example 3 — Same-Day Sick Appointments Ad spend: $600 New sick-pet cases: 10 Average visit revenue: $250 Total revenue: $2,500 **ROAS: 4.1× — for every $1 spent, you earned $4.10**

None of these examples include lifetime value — the returning wellness visits, dental cleanings, and annual exams that follow. Factor those in and every number above multiplies significantly.

A Note on Attribution

One thing worth being clear about: not every new client who walks through your door during an ad campaign can be traced directly back to that ad. Marketing rarely works in a perfectly straight line.

When you run a dental campaign, for example, you may see a meaningful increase in dental appointments. Some of those clients clicked your ad directly. Others saw the ad, mentioned it to a neighbor, and that neighbor came in. Others had been meaning to book for months and your ad simply reminded them at the right moment. A few may have searched your name after seeing the ad on Facebook, found you on Google, and booked through your website — showing up in your analytics as an "organic" visit rather than a paid one.

This is called the halo effect of advertising — the related growth that surrounds a campaign but isn't directly attributable to it. It's real, it's valuable, and it's one of the reasons the true return on ad spend is almost always higher than what the numbers show on paper.

What this means practically is this: don't evaluate your ad campaigns in isolation. Look at the broader picture. Are overall new client numbers up? Is production increasing in the service category you promoted? Are you hearing your clinic's name mentioned more often in the community? These are all signals that your advertising is working — even when every individual client can't be traced back to a single click.

Track what you can. Observe what you can't. And resist the temptation to judge an ad campaign purely on the clients who said "I found you on Google" — because the full picture is always bigger than that.

Measurement

Review a snapshot of your ad performance every month. This keeps you informed, helps you catch problems early, and gives you the data to make confident adjustments. At minimum, track:

- Total ad spend
- Leads generated
- Booked appointments
- New clients acquired (not returning ones)

These four numbers tell a clear story about whether your advertising is working and where to focus next.

Bringing It All Together

Ads create visibility on demand. Reviews create trust. Social media builds familiarity. Your website and service pages create clarity. Your team creates the experience that turns first visits into lifelong clients. When these parts support each other, growth stops feeling random and starts feeling repeatable.

Digital advertising isn't about shouting. It's about showing up — with the right message, in the right place, at the right time — and making it effortless for a pet owner to say yes.

Exercise For Your Clinic — 30 Minutes This Week

1. **Pick one** service to promote next month — dental, puppy/kitten packages, senior wellness, laser therapy, same-day sick care, or equine
2. **Write** the one-sentence promise in plain language: what it is, why it helps, and what happens next
3. **Confirm** you have — or create — a matching landing page on your website
4. **Allocate** a starter budget you're comfortable testing for

   30 days
5. **Decide** your success math upfront: target new clients, acceptable CAC, and the team member accountable for answering calls within three rings
6. **Launch** the campaign — or hand this plan to your agency with clear expectations

---

In the next chapter, we shift from attracting clients to converting them — and the front desk is where that conversion either happens or falls apart. You'll learn how to turn your team into one of your most powerful marketing assets.

PART THREE

LONG-TERM LOYALTY

Delivering Remarkable Experiences Before, During & After the Visit

Chapter Eight

THE FRONT OFFICE: WHERE MARKETING *SUCCEEDS OR FAILS*

"Without that exceptional front-line experience, even the best marketing efforts — your social media posts, stunning ads, and a visually compelling website — will ultimately fail to achieve their expected response."

— Dr. Joel Parker, DVM, and Leading Consultant to Independent Veterinary Clinics

While writing this book, I had a conversation with Dr. Christine Staten that cuts straight to the heart of this chapter:

"Your marketing can be flawless. Your medicine can be exceptional. But if a client walks in the door and feels invisible, rushed, or confused, none of that matters. The front desk is where client retention is won or lost — not in the exam room, not on the invoice — right there at that first hello."

Dr. Christine Staten is the owner and CEO of Adobe Veterinary Center in Arizona — a large dual-service practice with two interconnected divisions, small animal and equine, operating under her leadership with ten doctors and more than twenty staff members. A graduate with both a Doctor of Veterinary Medicine and a Master of Business Administration, Dr. Staten brings a rare combination of clinical proficiency and strategic vision to her role. She understands growth not just as a concept, but as an operational challenge that plays out in real time, every single day.

Everything we've discussed up to this point — message clarity, findability, trust-building social media, thoughtful advertising — serves one objective: to bring a client to your practice. to bring a client to your practice. What happens next determines whether that effort compounds into long-term growth or quietly disappears.

You've learned how pet owners find you, how they evaluate you, and why they decide to take action. You've seen how clarity in messaging, consistency in presence, and responsible advertising work together to generate demand.

But the moment a new client walks through your door, marketing steps aside. The front office takes over.

And clients make decisions faster than we'd like to admit.

As Dr. Staten puts it: *"Clients make up their minds about your practice before the doctor ever walks in the room. The energy, the eye contact, the genuine warmth at check-in is what sets the tone for everything that follows. You can't recover from a bad first impression with good medicine."*

This is an uncomfortable truth — but an important one.

A practice can deliver excellent care and still struggle with retention if the first human interaction feels disjointed, distracted, or transactional. Clients don't separate the front desk from the medical team. They experience your practice as one continuous relationship. By the time the doctor enters the room, the emotional tone has already been set.

The Moment Everything Becomes Real

From a client's perspective, the front office isn't a department. It is the practice. Let that sink in.

A lively, warm, and present front office professional can be the single greatest driver of growth in a practice. And the wrong person — someone disengaged, negative, or overwhelmed — can become a quiet handbrake that drains the energy and momentum from the entire team.

I've seen this play out in practices across the country. A client in Sarasota, Florida had a woman named Annette posted near the front door — someone who could have been anyone's grandmother. She was simply the greeter. That was her entire role. She was full of joy. Every client and every pet seemed to know her personally. She could name every single animal that walked through that door. The doctor told me (in front of her, of course) Annette was the single most valuable marketing asset in the entire clinic.

Marketing sets expectations. The front office decides whether those expectations get validated or betrayed.

And the better the marketing, the more critical the front office becomes.

Why? Because effective marketing doesn't just increase visibility — it increases pressure. More calls come in. More new clients arrive. Urgency rises. The pace picks up everywhere. These are good things — this is the productive pressure that drives growth. But if the front office isn't structured to absorb that pressure with calm, clarity, and presence, the practice starts to feel strained — and new clients notice immediately. They may feel unwelcome, or sense that you're simply too busy for them.

One of the most striking examples of getting this right comes from Dr. Staten's own practice:

"*One of the best decisions we ever made was removing our front desk team from incoming phone calls entirely. When someone walks through that door, they deserve 100% of that person's attention — not the back of someone's head while they're on hold. Presence is a practice value. And we protect it structurally.*"

FRONT-OFFICE BREAKDOWNS

Not all front-office breakdowns look dramatic. Most don't show up as complaints. Most don't result in confrontation. Most don't get mentioned at all. Instead, they show up weeks later as a client who never schedules again — or a family who quietly switches practices without explanation.

These breakdowns are subtle, cumulative, and expensive when measured against the lifetime value of a client. Here are two of the most common.

Breakdown #1: The Rushed First Contact

One of the most common — and most damaging — front-office failures happens during the very first interaction.

A new client calls. The phones are busy. The receptionist is multitasking. The tone is technically polite, but hurried. Instructions are fast. Details half-explained.

Nothing is wrong, exactly. But nothing is reassuring either.

I once worked with a practice that was convinced their marketing was attracting "the wrong kind of clients." They described new callers as price-sensitive, impatient, and uncommitted. They wanted clients with more discretionary income who were seeking top-quality medicine.

When my colleague Joel listened to their call recordings, something else was happening entirely. The front desk was efficient — but not orienting. New clients were being processed, not guided. Appointments were booked, but no emotional clarity was created. Questions were answered, but no confidence was built. Clients arrived already defensive, uncertain, and braced for friction.

Those first calls were setting the tone for disengagement — not because the medicine wasn't excellent, but because the relationship never fully formed.

Breakdown #2: Divided Attention at Check-In

Another quiet retention killer is divided presence.

A client walks in. The front desk staff is on the phone. Someone gestures vaguely toward a clipboard. Eye contact is brief or absent. The client sits down, unsure what to do next.

Nothing hostile. Nothing obviously wrong. But the experience communicates something unintended: You're not fully here for me. I'm not that important.

Clients either leave quietly, or complete their appointment and never return for follow-ups. I've seen practices where the marketing was working beautifully — ads were converting, new clients were calling consistently — but the moment they entered the building, momentum stalled. New clients didn't stick. Not because of the medicine. Because of the welcome.

Why These Moments Matter More Than Big Mistakes

What makes these breakdowns dangerous is that they feel minor to staff but feel significant to clients. In a world where genuine human connection is increasingly rare, walking into a business and feeling truly seen makes all the difference.

The front office is where clients decide:

- Whether they're allowed to ask questions
- Whether they're inconveniencing the team
- Whether they're welcome — or merely tolerated

Veterinary medicine is emotionally loaded. Pets are family. Fear is high. Guilt is often present. Clients walk in hoping someone will anchor them.

The good news is that these breakdowns can be fixed — and more easily than most practice owners expect. These are not personality problems. They are systems problems. They're about:

- How phones and foot traffic overlap
- How roles are structured
- How presence is protected
- How new clients are oriented into certainty

When practices fix these moments, call volume becomes less stressful. Front desk burnout decreases. Client trust accelerates. Marketing starts to feel easier — not because you're doing more, but because fewer people are falling through cracks you didn't realize were there.

Why This Chapter Comes After Advertising

This chapter doesn't follow digital advertising by coincidence. Advertising brings people to your practice. The front office determines whether they stay.

You can have strong ads and weak retention. You can generate demand and still leak growth. You can do everything right in marketing and wonder why it doesn't compound. When that happens, the issue is rarely visibility. It's experience.

In the sections that follow, we'll look closely at how the front office shapes outcomes — often in ways practices underestimate. We'll talk about tone, structure, first impressions, and the small decisions that create or erode trust.

Because when the front desk gets it right, everything that follows has a fighting chance. And when it doesn't — no amount of marketing can save it.

The Front Office As A Force Multiplier

Few people understand the true business impact of the front office better than someone who has spent decades inside practices and alongside the leaders who run them.

Dr. Joel Parker is a veterinarian and the founder of The Standing Ovation Practice™ — with more than 40 years spent coaching private practices across the country. When we spoke about the role of the front office in growth and retention, he offered a perspective that deserves to be read slowly and taken seriously.

What follows is Dr. Parker's observation, in his own words:

> *"In my 40+ years of coaching private practices, I cannot overstate the profound impact a truly excellent customer service representative (CSR) has on creating an 'above and beyond' customer experience — and the 'stickiness' that turns new clients into lifetime practice advocates.*
>
> *When you have such a person on your team, there's an undeniable magic to the initial client encounter. It exceeds expectations, leaving new clients not just satisfied, but excited to return and eager to wave your banner far and wide. Google reviews? They happen spontaneously — like standing ovations after an emotional, uplifting performance.*
>
> *Without that exceptional front-line experience, even the best marketing efforts — your social media posts, stunning ads, and visually compelling websites — ultimately fall flat. They draw people in, only for a bland, disappointing, or frustrating interaction to drive them away.*
>
> *The 'above expectations' experience exhilarates and builds loyalty. Anything less breeds disappointment and churn.*
>
> *So where do you find these magical CSRs? In my experience, only about 1 in 10 or 20 applicants truly fit the bill — they're rare,*

and the best ones are likely already working elsewhere.

A proven approach we've used successfully: start looking among your current clients walking through your front door. Many exceptional people are already in your practice as clients, waiting to be discovered and invited to join your team.

Once you have them — or if you're already blessed with one — compensate them generously. They are every bit as valuable as your technical and clinical staff.

Begin your search now. The effect these rare individuals have on your practice is profound: they supercharge the ROI of your marketing, create genuine buzz in both your physical community and online presence, and build the kind of loyalty that sustains long-term growth.

— Dr. Joel Parker Founder, The Standing Ovation Practice™

Dr. Parker's words bring us full circle.

Marketing creates interest. Advertising creates opportunity. The front office determines whether that opportunity becomes growth — or regret.

When the front office system is set up well, marketing efforts don't just perform — they compound. Reviews happen naturally. Referrals feel enthusiastic. Clients stay longer, trust faster, and advocate freely.

A Practice-Changing Exercise: Experience Your Practice Like A Client

This exercise is simple — but only works if you approach it with complete honesty. Stay patient. Don't rush to fix things as you go. This is an observation process first.

Step 1: Become a Stranger to Your Own Practice

- Pretend you've never heard of your practice. Then do the following:
- Search online for a vet the way a real pet owner would
- Visit your website on your phone — not a desktop
- Look at your Google profile and your reviews
- Scroll through your social media feeds
- Call your practice as if you were a new client

As you do this, don't ask: ***"Is this good?"***

Ask instead:

- Does this look like a practice I'd feel comfortable bringing my pet to?
- Do I feel calm, or rushed?
- Do I feel guided, or confused?
- Do I feel genuinely welcomed?
- Write everything down — without defending yourself.

Step 2: Shadow the Front Office for Two Hours

Spend 2 hours observing front-office interactions. Not to correct. Not to judge. Just to listen and watch.

Pay attention to:

- Tone on the phone
- Body language at check-in
- Eye contact
- How questions are answered
- What happens when things get busy

Ask yourself: ***If this were my first interaction with this practice, would it confirm the trust our marketing promises?***

If the answer is "sometimes" — you've just found a significant opportunity.

Step 3: Ask One Honest Question

At the end of the week, bring your team together and ask one question:

"If you were a new client, where would you feel most uncertain or overwhelmed?"

Then listen. Without interruption. Without explanation. Without defense.

Your team already knows where most of the gaps are. They live them every single day. Take notes and take them seriously.

Step 4: Pick One Thing to Improve — Not Ten

Don't overhaul everything at once. Pick one moment in the client journey to improve:

- A clearer, warmer phone script
- A calmer, more attentive check-in process
- Better handoffs between the front office and medical staff
- A structural change that protects presence — as Dr. Staten described

And ask yourself: what foundational marketing factors also need attention — website clarity, social media consistency, Google profile accuracy?

Small shifts create disproportionate impact. One fixed moment in the client journey can change the entire experience of your practice.

Final Thought

Marketing gets attention. Advertising creates opportunities. And the experience inside your door creates loyalty.

Practices that grow well don't just attract clients. They make people feel confident they chose correctly — for themselves and for the animals they love.

If there's one idea to carry forward from this chapter, it's this: growth is not about doing more. It's about aligning what you promise with what people experience. When those two things align — your practice stops grinding, the momentum builds on its own, and you're finally flying.

In the next chapter, we'll look at what happens after that first great experience — and how to build the systems that keep clients coming back for life.

Chapter Nine

LOYALTY: HOW PRACTICES WIN THE LONG GAME

> *"There is only one boss. The customer. And he can fire everybody in the company from the chairman on down, simply by spending his money somewhere else."*
>
> — Sam Walton, Founder of Walmart

While this book has focused on building a system that consistently brings new clients into your practice, the true long-term win comes from something deeper: loyalty.

Loyalty is what happens when a client decides — consciously or not — "This is our practice." Not just a veterinarian. Not simply the nearest clinic. But our place. Our people. Our practice.

And loyal clients are also your best ambassadors — a point worth remembering every time you're tempted to focus all your energy on finding new clients while the ones you already have quietly drift away.

Loyalty reduces friction everywhere. Yet it is rarely managed intentionally. Practices — much like the early stages of building any business — often focus heavily on how clients enter but spend far less time considering why they stay for ten years or more, bringing every new pet they adopt back to you without ever questioning the choice.

That's the long game. And it's worth playing deliberately. Clients stay loyal when:

- They feel guided, not judged
- They feel their concerns are taken seriously — even the ones that seem small
- They receive personal attention — an unexpected check-in or follow-up call that reminds them they matter beyond the transaction

Veterinary clients don't remember every clinical detail of every visit. But they remember how they felt being cared for. That emotional memory is what brings them back — and what they share with others.

On the flip side, loyalty often erodes not from a single bad experience, but from a slow accumulation of being made to feel routine. When familiarity quietly becomes complacency — when clients begin to feel rushed, overlooked, or handled with less care because they're no longer new — something shifts. Subconsciously, they begin to wonder whether they might be better appreciated somewhere else. An emergency happens. They try another clinic. And from the practice's perspective, they "just stopped coming." From the client's perspective, the relationship simply faded.

This is one of the most common — and most preventable — sources of practice attrition.

Trust Over Time Creates Permission

This is one of the most important concepts in this entire book — and one of the least discussed but most "understood" in veterinary marketing.

Clients who have been with a practice for years demonstrate a fundamentally different kind of trust than new clients. They accept thoughtful recommendations with far less hesitation. They ask fewer defensive questions. They extend good faith more readily — because that good faith has been earned, consistently, over time.

The deeper the loyalty, the more permission clients grant. Permission to recommend higher-value care. Permission to guide difficult decisions. Permission to lead rather than sell.

Loyal clients rarely accuse a practice of "upselling." They've internalized your intentions. They trust your judgment because it has been proven — appointment after appointment, year after year, pet after pet.

That trust must be cultivated deliberately. It cannot be rushed. But it can be built — through systems, through consistency, and through the kind of genuine care that clients feel every time they walk through your door.

> *"Client loyalty in a veterinary practice isn't something that magically happens to you – it begins with selecting a staff of like-minded individuals that treat every client like family from the moment they walk through the door. With that foundation, what happens over time is something remarkable. We become part of their extended family too. They call us when they're worried at midnight. They bring us holiday cards. They introduce us to their grandchildren's first puppy. The clients who have been with us the longest aren't just our most valuable clients financially. They're our most forgiving, our most trusting, and our most vocal advocates in the community. They've seen us at our best and carried us through our hardest seasons. That kind of relationship doesn't come from great marketing alone. It comes from showing up for people – and their animals – in a hundred small ways they never forget."*
>
> – Dr. Kim Stewart, College Hills Veterinary Hospital, College Station, TX

Simple Systems That Build Loyalty

Building loyalty doesn't require a complex program or expensive software. It requires consistency — showing up for your clients in small, meaningful ways between visits. Here are the systems that make the biggest difference.

The New Client Welcome Sequence

The first thirty days after a new client's initial visit are the most important window in the entire client relationship. This is when impressions are freshest, habits are forming, and a simple gesture of follow-through can turn a first-time visitor into a long-term advocate.

A basic welcome sequence looks like this:

- A personal follow-up call or text within 24 hours of the first visit — *"How is [pet name] doing today?"*
- A personally signed welcome letter — mailed within the first week. In a digital-first world, an actual piece of mail from a local business is a rare and memorable gesture. It doesn't need to be long. It just needs to be warm and real. You can download a ready-to-use welcome letter template at **cebronwalker.com/free-resources**
- A welcome email within the first week that introduces your team, outlines your services, and shares what to expect from your practice
- A thirty-day check-in — brief, warm, and genuine — that simply says: "We're glad you found us."

None of these require significant time. All of them communicate something powerful: you matter to us beyond the appointment.

Preventive Care Reminders

Clients want to do right by their pets — they simply need reminding. A consistent cadence of seasonal reminders, vaccine due dates, and annual wellness prompts keeps your practice top of mind and helps clients stay proactive rather than reactive.

When a client receives a timely, personalized reminder — especially one that mentions their pet by name and references their specific care history — it communicates that your practice is paying attention. That attention is one of the quietest and most effective loyalty builders available to you.

The Follow-Up Call After Significant Visits

After a surgery, a serious diagnosis, a dental procedure, or any visit that carried emotional weight for the client, a follow-up call the next day is one of the most powerful things your team can do. It costs minutes. It communicates volumes.

Clients who receive unexpected follow-up calls after significant visits are significantly more likely to leave detailed, positive reviews — and to refer others. Not because you asked them to, but because that level of care genuinely surprised them. And surprise, in a good way, is one of the most memorable things a practice can deliver.

Birthday and Milestone Acknowledgments

A simple message on a pet's birthday — or on the anniversary of their adoption — costs nothing and creates a moment of genuine delight. These touchpoints are easy to automate through most practice management systems and keep your practice present in a client's life during the long stretches between visits.

Educational Content That Keeps Clients Engaged

Blogs, short videos, seasonal tips, and social posts that answer the questions your clients ask most often serve a dual purpose: they help clients make better decisions for their pets, and they remind clients that your practice is a trusted resource — not just a destination for emergencies.

The practices that grow most naturally are the ones clients think of first — not just when something is wrong, but when they have a question, when a friend needs a recommendation, or when a new pet enters the family.

Loyalty Turns Marketing into Momentum

Here's where everything in this book connects — where the flywheel truly begins to turn.

Loyalty closes the loop on every marketing investment you make. Loyal clients become:

- **Review generators** — they leave detailed, enthusiastic Google reviews because their experience has genuinely earned it
- **Referral engines** — they send friends, neighbors, coworkers, and anyone in their social circle who mentions needing a vet
- **Brand defenders** — they respond to negative online comments, share your posts, and speak up for your practice in community groups
- **Stabilizers** — they provide steady, predictable revenue during slower seasons and help cushion the impact of unpredictable periods

Practices with strong loyalty spend more efficiently on advertising. They grow steadily instead of spiking and crashing. They feel calmer — even during busy or stressful seasons — because their foundation is stable.

Marketing attracts attention. Loyalty creates momentum. And loyalty doesn't replace marketing — it multiplies its effectiveness. Every new client your marketing brings in becomes exponentially more valuable when your practice is built to retain them.

Loyalty Self Assessment: Five Questions Worth Asking

Grab your pencil and answer these five questions honestly about your practice right now:

1. Do new clients receive a personal follow-up contact within 24 hours of their first visit? *(Yes / Sometimes / Not yet)*
2. Does your team know each returning client, and their pet, by name before they reach the front desk? *(Yes / Sometimes / Not yet)*
3. Do clients receive a follow-up call after significant procedures or difficult diagnoses? *(Yes / Sometimes / Not yet)*
4. Are preventive care reminders sent on a consistent, personalized schedule — or only when someone remembers? *(Consistent / Inconsistent / Not in place)*
5. When a client hasn't been in for more than 18 months, does your practice have a system to reach out — or do they simply disappear? *(System in place / Ad hoc / No system)*

Any "Sometimes," "Not yet," or "No system" answer is an opportunity. Pick one and fix it this month. Loyalty is built one small system at a time.

When the Experience Matches the Promise

This book has never been about tactics in isolation. It has been about sequence, alignment, and integrity.

You've learned that effective growth doesn't begin with ads. It begins with clarity — about who you serve, how you serve them, and what makes your practice worth trusting. You've seen how findability ensures the right people can discover you. How social presence builds familiarity before urgency. How advertising captures intent without manipulation. And how the front office either confirms or contradicts everything your marketing promised.

The truth is straightforward: pet owners don't judge your practice by your intentions. They judge it by their experience. Your marketing creates a promise. Your front office confirms whether that promise is real. Your team, your systems, and your consistency determine whether a first-time client becomes a lifelong one.

When those things align — trust compounds. Growth becomes sustainable. Loyalty becomes natural. And your practice stops feeling like it's constantly grinding just to keep pace.

When they don't align, no amount of traffic, ads, or tactics will save it.

The good news is this: alignment is a choice. And when alignment is built into a system — not reliant on individual effort alone — growth becomes repeatable. Predictable. And far more enjoyable to be part of.

In the next chapter, we'll bring everything together — the complete flywheel system that ties every part of this book into one clear, connected model for practice growth. Because understanding each piece individually is valuable. But seeing how they all work together is what changes everything.

Chapter Ten

THE OWNER/MANAGER FLYWHEEL SYSTEM

"Marketing's job is never done. It's about perpetual motion. We must continue to innovate every day."

— Beth Comstock, Chief Marketing Officer, General Electric

At this point, you've noticed that none of the ideas we've discussed stand alone. Messaging doesn't work without trust. Trust doesn't scale without systems. Advertising doesn't perform without clarity. And loyalty doesn't happen by accident.

What creates sustainable growth in a veterinary practice is not a single tactic — it's alignment across time. That's why I believe growth is more like a flywheel. It has a sequence, but once it's moving, it builds energy and momentum to keep itself going.

Healthy practices grow over time by building exactly that kind of momentum. The flywheel gives us something to not only understand but to see clearly — a system that, once in motion, requires less force to keep going, not more.

If you've sat at a potter's wheel, you know that sensation. That large, heavy concrete wheel — once you get it moving, the energy becomes difficult to slow down. A small push from your foot keeps it going effortlessly. That's what we want your marketing to feel like.

A practice that jumps from tactic to tactic — trying this platform, then that campaign, then the next new idea — will scramble every month without building anything lasting. I've been doing this a long time and have seen every version of it. A practice that works through each step covered in this book, and gets this marketing flywheel moving, grows calmly — even during uncertain or challenging periods.

The Flywheel in Business

The flywheel concept isn't new — but one of the most powerful real-world applications comes from a business you know well: Amazon.

Jeff Bezos famously sketched his original vision on a napkin — not as a linear plan or sequence, but as a circle. At the center was customer experience. Better customer experience led to more traffic. More traffic attracted more third-party sellers. More sellers increased selection. Greater selection allowed for lower prices through scale and efficiency. Lower prices, in turn, improved the customer experience even further. Then the cycle started again — spinning faster each time.

What made this idea so powerful wasn't any single tactic — pricing, fulfillment, or technology — but how each element reinforced the others. Every improvement fed the next. Over time, the flywheel built momentum. Amazon didn't rely on constant bursts of advertising to survive. The system itself generated growth. Once the flywheel was in motion, every satisfied customer became energy for the next rotation.

This is the mindset we're building in your practice.

And here's something worth understanding about the world your clients are living in right now. Customers aren't only looking at your website or your YouTube videos to decide whether you're the right veterinarian for their pets. Third-party review sites, recommendations from friends, real client testimonials on social media — these things play a bigger role in buying decisions than ever before.

At the same time, overall trust in businesses is declining. HubSpot has reported that 81% of customers trust recommendations from family and friends more than advice from businesses directly — and 55% say they trust the businesses they buy from less than they used to. That's a significant shift. And it's exactly why a system built on genuine trust, consistent experience, and real human connection is more powerful today than any single marketing tactic could ever be.

In the past, potential clients had to speak with you directly to gather information, or find a friend who knew you personally. Today, the access everyone has is completely different. People ask their networks for advice, search for mentions of your practice on social media, and read third-party reviews on Google — often before they've ever visited your website.

A flywheel marketing model brings all of these forces together, working in your favor, building on each other over time.

Your practice grows by creating an experience so clear, helpful, and trustworthy that each touchpoint — your website, your reviews, your social media, your ads, your appointments, your patient care, your follow-ups — feeds the next.

THE VETERINARY PRACTICE GROWTH FLYWHEEL

Here is the system you've built throughout this book, viewed as a complete flywheel.

This model builds on a well-established marketing framework — adapted here specifically for veterinary practice growth.

On the outside of the flywheel are three large organizing concepts that capture the full arc of the client relationship:

- **Attract** — drawing the right clients to your practice

- **Engage** — building familiarity, trust, and demand
- **Delight** — delivering experiences that create loyalty and fuel the cycle again

Moving inward, we find the seven-step process that powers each of those three phases — each piece building on the last, over and over, accumulating momentum.

1. Message–Market Fit

Everything begins here. You define clearly who you serve and what matters to them. Your messaging speaks directly to real client needs, addresses emotional concerns, and differentiates your practice in ways that are meaningful — not generic. Clarity at this stage reduces confusion everywhere else.

2. Findability

Once your message is clear, you ensure the right people can find you at the moment they need help — through local search, a complete and active Google Business Profile, AI visibility, and a humanized website that speaks their language. Visibility only works when it reflects clarity.

3. Trust Signals

Reviews, testimonials, real imagery, and consistent tone all reinforce the same story: this practice is credible, competent, and genuinely human. Trust is not claimed — it is demonstrated, repeatedly, over time.

4. Social Presence & Community Awareness

Social media and community presence allow clients to observe your practice long before urgency sets in. They learn how you think, how you communicate, what your culture feels like, and how you care. Familiarity lowers resistance. When the moment of need arrives, they already know you.

5. Demand Capture — Advertising

Advertising places your practice in front of pet owners who are already looking for help. When aligned with everything above, advertising feels helpful rather than pushy. Ads don't create demand — they meet it at exactly the right moment.

6. Front Office Experience

The front desk confirms whether the promises made by your marketing are real. Presence, clarity, warmth, and structure determine whether trust locks in or quietly unravels. This is where growth compounds — or where it leaks.

7. Loyalty

Through consistent experiences, clear communication, and aligned values, clients choose to stay. They return. They refer. They review. They bring their next animal — and their neighbor's animal — back to you. Loyalty multiplies everything that came before it.

The Flywheel in Action

And then — critically — the cycle feeds back on itself.

Loyal clients generate reviews. Reviews strengthen trust signals. Stronger trust improves advertising performance. Better ad performance brings in more of the right clients. More of the right clients create calmer, more confident operations. And calmer operations allow your team to deliver the kind of experience that generates loyalty all over again.

The flywheel spins faster — with less effort — each time it completes a rotation.

What This Means for Practice Owners and Managers

You do not need to do everything at once — and you certainly don't need to do it in perfect order. But you do need to understand one important principle: frustration comes when you ask one part of the system to do the job of another.

Social posts cannot do the work of ads. Ads cannot compensate for a weak website that hasn't been humanized. Reviews cannot make up for a poor front office experience. Each part of the flywheel has a specific role — and when you respect that role, the whole system becomes easier to manage, not harder.

How to Use This Book Going Forward

This book is not meant to be read once and shelved. It is a diagnostic tool — one that becomes more useful over time as your practice grows and evolves.

Different chapters become relevant at different seasons of your practice:

- **Struggling to convert new inquiries into booked appointments?** Revisit Chapter 3 — Message–Market Fit — and Chapter 8 — Front Office Experience
- **Spending on ads without seeing results?** Check trust signals and website clarity first — Chapters 4 and 5 — before adjusting your campaigns
- **Seeing client churn or team burnout?** Look at Chapter 8 on front office systems and Chapter 9 on loyalty — the answers are usually there
- **Not showing up in local search or AI recommendations?** Return to Chapter 4 and review your online foundation, Google Business Profile, and AI visibility

When something feels stuck, ask yourself: which part of the flywheel isn't aligned right now? The answer will point you to the chapter you need.

A Final Thought

You picked up this book because you care about building something that lasts. That's exactly the kind of practice owner this system was built for.

Successful veterinary practice growth is not loud. It is not frantic. It is not built on the next shiny tactic or the biggest ad budget.

When what you say, how you show up, how clients are treated, and how care is delivered all tell the same story — growth becomes natural. Not something you force. Something that flows.

To your success.

It is built with alignment.

It is built by being more human.

APPENDIX A

Ideal Client Persona Builder

Survey + Worksheet

How to Use This Worksheet

This worksheet is designed to help you build a clear, practical persona for each of your primary client groups. Don't overthink it. The goal isn't a perfect profile — it's a usable one. Work through one persona at a time, answer each question as honestly as you can, and use what you build here to sharpen your website, your ads, your social media, and the way your front desk speaks to new clients.

Complete one worksheet per client segment. Most practices will identify two to three primary personas.

STEP 1 — Name Your Persona

Give your ideal client a first name, like "Jennifer" or "Cody". This makes the persona feel as if we're describing a real person. This keeps your team grounded when creating content or handling calls.

Persona name: ______________________________

Pet type / species: ______________________________

Primary service they need: ______________________________

STEP 2 — What Do They Want?

What is the primary outcome this client is looking for when they search for a veterinarian?

____

____

What does a great experience look like to them?

____

____

STEP 3 — What Do They Worry About?

What fears or frustrations might hold them back from booking or switching vets?

- ______________________________
- ______________________________
- ______________________________

STEP 4 — How Do They Search?

What words or phrases would they type into Google when looking for a practice like yours?

- ______________________________
- ______________________________

- ______________________________

Where else do they look beyond Google? (circle all that apply)

Google Maps   Facebook Groups   Instagram   Nextdoor   YouTube

Word of Mouth   Referral from another professional

STEP 5 — What Helps Them Choose?

Rank the following from 1 (most important) to 6 (least important) for this persona:

___ Google reviews and star rating

___ Social media posts on Instagram / Facebook / TikTok

___ Photos of the team and clinic

___ Website clarity and ease of booking

___ Availability and response time

___ Species-specific expertise

___ Price and payment options

STEP 6 — Write Their Key Message

Using what you've learned above, write one sentence that speaks directly to this persona — the message that would make them feel immediately understood.

____

“____

____”

STEP 7 — Gut Check

Answer these three questions honestly:

Does your current website speak directly to this persona?
Yes / Somewhat / No

Do your Google reviews reflect the experience this persona is looking for? Yes / Somewhat / No

Would this persona feel immediately at home calling your front desk? Yes / Somewhat / No

Any “Somewhat” or “No” answers are your starting points.

Use one worksheet per persona. Get additional copies of the worksheet at **cebronwalker.com/free-resources**. Or scan the QR Code below. Get these done and improve your marketing — your personas shape all marketing decisions from here forward.

Scan Me!

APPENDIX B

Front Desk Call Handling Playbook

Why Speed Is Everything

Speed-to-lead is how fast your practice responds when a potential new client reaches out. A new inquiry responded to within five minutes is dramatically more likely to convert into a booked appointment than one responded to an hour later — or worse, the next day! The client's urgency doesn't wait, and if they don't get a response quickly, and they're stressed, they are going to call your competitor.

Response Standards Every Practice Should Meet

- Phone call (incoming): Answer within 3 rings
- Web form submission: Personal response within 30 minutes
- Text message: Response within 15 minutes
- After-hours inquiry: Auto-acknowledgment immediately, plus personal follow-up the next morning
- Missed call from a new client: Return the call within 30 minutes
- No booking after the first call: Follow up on Day 2 and Day 5
- After a first visit: Personal follow-up call within 24 hours
- After a significant procedure: Personal follow-up call the next morning

The Phone Call Framework: Welcome, Listen, Guide, Book

Every new client phone call should follow four steps. These steps work for any scenario — urgent sick visits, wellness inquiries, price questions, or new client calls.

Step 1 — Welcome

Answer with warmth and confidence. Every time. The first three seconds set the emotional tone for the entire call.

"Thank you for calling [Practice Name] — this is [Your Name]. How can I help you today?"

Never answer mid-conversation with a colleague. The client deserves your full attention from the first word.

Step 2 — Listen

Let the client tell you why they're calling without interrupting. People need to feel heard — especially when they're worried about a pet. After they've explained, reflect it back:

"I understand — [pet name] has been [brief summary of concern]. I want to make sure we get them the right care."

This one step communicates more warmth and competence than almost anything else you can do on a call.

Step 3 — Guide

Once you understand their need, guide them toward the right next step. One clear path forward — don't overwhelm with options.

For a sick pet: *"We do have availability for a sick visit — I'd love to get [pet name] in to see one of our doctors. Can I find you a time today or tomorrow?"*

For a wellness visit: *"Absolutely — let's get [pet name] set up for a wellness exam. I have a few openings this week. What days work best for you?"*

For a new client who isn't sure: *"I'd love to tell you a little about how we work — and then we can find a time that makes sense. Does that sound okay?"*

Step 4 — Book

Always end the call with a booked appointment or a clear next step. Never let a new client call end with "just give us a call when you're ready." That's a lost client.

"Can I take your name and number so I can follow up with you tomorrow? I want to make sure you're taken care of."

Then follow up. Tomorrow. Without fail.

CALL SCRIPTS BY SCENARIO

New Client — First Call

"Thank you for calling [Practice Name] — this is [Name]. How can I help you today?"

[Client explains they're looking for a new vet]

"Wonderful — we'd love to welcome you. Do you have a specific concern today, or are you looking for a practice for ongoing care?"

[Guide based on their answer, then:]

"Let me get you set up as a new client — this will just take a moment. Can I get your name and your pet's name?"

Sick Pet — Urgent Call

Never make an urgent caller feel like a burden. Their fear is real. Your calm confidence is the reassurance they need.

"Thank you for calling [Practice Name] — this is [Name]. How can I help you today?"

[Client explains pet is unwell]

"I'm glad you called. Let me make sure we get [pet name] seen as soon as possible. Can you tell me a little more about what you're noticing?"

[Listen, then:]

"We can get you in [today / this morning / this afternoon]. Does [time] work for you?"

Price Question Before Booking

This is one of the most common moments where confidence wavers. Here's how to handle it:
"That's a great question — our exam fees start at [amount]. Depending on what [pet name] needs, the doctor will walk you through any recommendations and costs before anything is done. There are never any surprises. Would you like to get an appointment scheduled?"

Acknowledge the question. Give a general answer. Redirect to booking. Don't apologize for your prices.

Missed Call — New Client Voicemail

Return the call within 30 minutes. If you reach voicemail:
"Hi, this is [Name] calling from [Practice Name] — I'm returning your call from earlier today. We'd love to help you and [pet name]. Please give us a call back at [number] — we're open until [time] today. Looking forward to speaking with you."

If they don't call back, try once more the following morning.

After-Hours Inquiry — Automated Response

Set this up as an automated text or email for any inquiry received outside business hours:

"Thank you for reaching out to [Practice Name]. We've received your message and one of our team members will be in touch with you first thing tomorrow morning. If this is an emergency, please contact [local emergency vet name and number]. We look forward to speaking with you soon."

Managing Two Calls — When You're Handling an Emergency

Small practices often run with one person at the front desk. When an emergency call comes in while you're already on the line, keep it simple.

Placing a caller on hold: *"I'm so sorry — I have an urgent situation. Can I place you on a brief hold, or call you right back in two minutes?"*

Returning to the caller on hold: *"Thank you so much for waiting — now, how can I help you?"*

When a new call comes in during an emergency, let it go to voicemail. Return it within 15 minutes:

"Hi — this is [Name] from [Practice Name]. Sorry I missed you. How can I help?"

Never put an emergency caller on hold for a new inquiry. A new client who gets a warm callback within 15 minutes will almost always still book. An emergency caller who feels abandoned won't come back.

Follow-Up Workflows

Most practices lose new clients not because they gave a bad first impression — but because they didn't follow up at all. Here is the follow-up sequence every practice should have in place.

New Inquiry — Follow-Up Sequence

- **Immediately:** Acknowledge the inquiry — phone, text, or automated message
- **Within 30 minutes:** Personal response from a team member during business hours
- **Day 2 (if no booking):** One follow-up call or text — warm, not pushy
- **Day 5 (if still no booking):** Final follow-up — brief, friendly, no pressure

Day 2 script: *"Hi [Client Name] — this is [Name] from [Practice Name]. I just wanted to follow up and see if you had any questions or if you'd like to get [pet name] scheduled. We're here whenever you're ready."*

Day 5 script: *"Hi [Client Name] — just a friendly note from [Practice Name]. We'd love to help with [pet name]'s care whenever the time is right. Feel free to reach out anytime."*

After Day 5, let it go gracefully. A third or fourth follow-up risks leaving a negative impression.

Post-Visit Follow-Up — New Client

Within 24 hours: .*"Hi [Client Name] — this is [Name] from [Practice Name]. I just wanted to check in and see how [pet name] is doing after their visit yesterday. Please don't hesitate to reach out if you have any questions."*

Most clients have never received a follow-up call from a veterinary practice. The ones who do remember it for years.

Post-Significant-Visit Follow-Up

Next morning: *"Hi [Client Name] — this is [Name] from [Practice Name]. I'm calling to check in on [pet name] after [procedure/visit] yesterday. How are they doing? Is there anything we can help you with?"*

You're not calling to upsell. You're calling because you care. Clients feel that distinction immediately.

Role-Play Guide for Team Training

Scripts only work when they feel natural — not rehearsed. The best way to get there is role-play. Set aside twenty minutes at a team meeting or weekly huddle.

How to Run a Session

- One team member plays the new client — use a real scenario from the past week
- One team member plays the front desk — uses the scripts as a guide, not verbatim
- The rest of the team observes and notes what felt warm, hesitant, or could be smoother
- Rotate roles and repeat

What to Listen For

- Did the greeting feel warm and confident?
- Was the client given a chance to fully explain before being interrupted?
- Was their concern reflected back before moving to a solution?
- Was a clear next step offered — not just information?
- Was an appointment booked, or a follow-up committed to?

Front Desk Daily Checklist

Start every day with this two-minute check:

- Any after-hours web forms or text inquiries to respond to from last night?
- Any missed calls from yesterday with no callback yet?
- Any Day 2 or Day 5 follow-ups due today?
- Any post-visit follow-up calls to make this morning?
- Phone lines tested and working correctly?
- Any voicemails from overnight to return?

Get additional copies of this Front Desk Call Handling Playbook at **cebronwalker.com/free-resources**. Or scan the QR Code below.

Scan Me!

APPENDIX C

AI Prompt Library for Veterinary Clinics

Ready-to-use prompts for ChatGPT, Claude, and other AI tools

How to Use This Library

Artificial intelligence tools like ChatGPT, Claude, and Google Gemini can save your practice significant time on writing, planning, and communication tasks. But the quality of what AI produces depends almost entirely on how clearly you ask — and how well the AI understands who you are before you start.

A Note on Paid vs. Free AI Tools

While free versions of AI tools can absolutely get you started, a paid subscription is worth the investment for a practice that plans to use AI regularly. Paid plans typically offer longer conversation memory, access to more capable models, fewer usage limits, and more consistent quality — all of which matter when you're using AI weekly for website copy, social posts scripts and ideas, and client communication. For the cost of a few cups of coffee a month, a paid plan removes the frustration of hitting limits mid-task and generally produces noticeably better writing.

A Note on AI's Tendency to Agree With You

Here's something worth knowing before you start: AI chat tools can be remarkably agreeable. If you tell an AI that your new tagline idea is brilliant and ask what it thinks, there's a good chance it will tell you it's brilliant too — even if it isn't. AI tools are designed to be helpful and accommodating, which means they can easily become a "yes man" if you let them.

You don't need that. You need honest, useful feedback.

When you want genuine feedback rather than validation, ask for it directly: "Give me your honest, unbiased opinion on this — including any weaknesses." Or simply present an idea without telling the AI how you feel about it first. The more neutral your prompt, the more useful and honest the response will be. Save the encouragement for your team — use AI for clear thinking.

Step 1 — Teach the AI About Your Practice First

Before using any prompt in this library, start every new AI session by pasting in what we call a Practice Context Prompt. This tells the AI who you are, who you serve, and how you communicate — so every piece of content it produces is tailored to your practice from the very first response.

Copy the template below, fill in your details, and paste it at the start of every new conversation before using any other prompt:

> *"Before we begin, I want to give you some background about my veterinary practice so that everything you write for me is accurate, on-brand, and specific to us.*

Practice name: [Practice Name]

Location: [City, State]

Years in business: [X years]

Number of doctors: [X]

Number of staff: [X]

Species and services we specialize in: [e.g., small animal — dogs and cats; exotic pets including rabbits, reptiles, and birds; equine and farm animal medicine; fear-free handling; urgent and same-day sick visits; dental care; laser therapy; etc.]

Our ideal clients are: [describe your ideal client — e.g., dog and cat owners in our suburban community who value relationship-based medicine, follow care recommendations, and want a practice they can trust for life.]

What makes us different from other practices in our area: [e.g., we offer same-day sick visits, we are a fear-free certified practice, we have two exotic-trained doctors on staff, etc.]

Our tone of voice is: warm, approachable, and trustworthy. We speak to clients like intelligent adults who love their animals — not down to them. We avoid medical jargon whenever possible.

Our community: [Describe your community — e.g., we serve a suburban community of approximately 80,000 people in the greater [City] area. We sponsor the local shelter and many of our clients have been with us for over a decade.]

Please use this information as the foundation for everything you write for me today. Always write in our voice, always keep our ideal client in mind, and always make content feel like it came from us — not from a generic veterinary practice."

A few tips before you start:

- Paste your Practice Context Prompt at the beginning of every new session — AI tools don't remember previous conversations. With paid accounts, you simply need to remind the AI that you want it to use the agreed on practice prompt.
- Always review and personalize AI output before publishing or sending.
- If the first result isn't quite right, simply say "Try again, but make it warmer" or "Make it shorter."
- Never publish AI-generated content without reading it carefully first.

SECTION 1 — Google Business Profile

Business Description

"Write a Google Business Profile description for [Practice Name] in [City, State]. We offer [list key services]. We have been serving the community for [X] years and are known for [key differentiator]. Keep it under 750 characters, include our city name naturally, and end with an invitation to call or book online."

Google Update — Service Promotion

A "Google Update" is a short post that appears directly on your Google Business Profile — similar to a social media post, but it shows up when someone finds you on Google Search or Maps.

"Write a Google Business Profile update promoting our [service — e.g., dental cleaning month, senior wellness exam] at [Practice Name] in [City]. Keep it under 150 words. Use a warm, friendly tone. End with a clear call to action — call us or book online."

Google Update — Team Highlight

"Write a warm, conversational Google Business Profile update introducing [team member name], [their role] at [Practice Name]. Include [one or two details about them]. Keep it under 100 words and end with a welcoming line for new clients."

Response to a Positive Review

"Write a warm, genuine response to this five-star Google review for [Practice Name]: '[paste review text here].' Keep it under 75 words. Thank the client by first name if mentioned. Reference their pet or the specific service if mentioned. Do not sound scripted or generic."

Response to a Negative Review

"Write a professional, calm response to this negative Google review for [Practice Name]: '[paste review text here].' Acknowledge their concern without admitting fault or revealing any client details. Keep it under 75 words. Stay warm and professional. Invite them to contact us directly to resolve the situation."

SECTION 2 — Website Copy

Homepage Headline

"Write three homepage headline options for a veterinary clinic called [Practice Name] in [City, State]. We specialize in [specialty]. Our tone is warm, approachable, and trustworthy. Each headline should be one sentence and speak directly to a pet owner's desire for compassionate, high-quality care."

About Us Page

"Write an About Us page for [Practice Name] in [City, State]. We have been serving the community for [X] years. Our team includes [number] doctors and [number] staff. Our philosophy is [brief description]. Write in a warm, human tone that helps pet owners feel they are choosing a practice that genuinely cares about them and their animals."

FAQ Section

This works well at the bottom of any service page on your website — three to five questions answered briefly builds trust and helps both pet owners and AI search tools understand your services clearly.

"Write five frequently asked questions and answers for the [service] page of a veterinary clinic website. The questions should reflect what a worried or first-time pet owner would actually ask. Keep answers brief, clear, and reassuring. Avoid medical jargon. The practice is called [Practice Name] and is located in [City, State]."

SECTION 3 — Social Media

Educational Post — General

"Write a social media post for [Practice Name] in [City] explaining [topic — e.g., why annual dental cleanings matter, signs your cat is in pain]. Write it for Facebook and Instagram. Keep it under 150 words, use plain language a non-medical person would understand, and end with a question or call to action that encourages engagement."

Behind-the-Scenes Post

"Write a warm, conversational social media caption for a behind-the-scenes photo at [Practice Name]. The photo shows [describe the photo — e.g., our team celebrating a patient's recovery, our front desk team laughing together]. Keep it under 100 words. Make it feel real and human — not like an ad."

Patient Success Story

Use this when you have a real story to share — either as a written post with a photo, or as the caption underneath a short video testimonial from the client. Briefly describe what happened in your own words, and let AI help you turn it into a polished, shareable post.

"Write a social media post sharing a patient success story for [Practice Name]. Here's what happened: [describe in your own words what the pet came in for and how it turned out — e.g., 'A dog named Max came in unable to walk on his back leg. After surgery and a few weeks of recovery, he's back to running at the park.']. Write it in a warm, storytelling tone. Keep it under 150 words. End with a line that invites pet owners to trust us with their animals."

Seasonal or Holiday Post

"Write a fun, warm social media post for [Practice Name] for [holiday or season — e.g., the start of summer, National Dog Day]. Include a brief pet health tip related to that time of year. Keep it under 100 words and end with a light call to action."

Reels or Short Video Script

"Write a 30-second script for a veterinary clinic reel or short video for [Practice Name]. The topic is [e.g., what to expect at your puppy's first visit, how we handle anxious cats]. The doctor or team member will speak directly to camera. Keep the tone warm, conversational, and simple. No medical jargon. End with a clear call to action."

SECTION 4 — Email & Client Communication

New Client Welcome Email

"Write a welcome email for a new client at [Practice Name] in [City]. They just brought in their [species] for the first time. Thank them for choosing us. Briefly introduce what to expect from our practice. Include our hours, phone number, and website. Keep the tone warm and personal — under 200 words."

Appointment Reminder

"Write a friendly appointment reminder text message for [Practice Name]. The client's name is [Name] and their pet's name is [Pet Name]. Their appointment is on [date] at [time]. Keep it under 60 words. Include a line asking them to call if they need to reschedule."

Post-Visit Follow-Up

"Write a follow-up text message from [Practice Name] to check in on a patient named [pet name] who visited yesterday for [service or reason]. Keep it warm, brief, and genuine — under 50 words."

Re-Engagement Email — Lapsed Client

"Write a re-engagement email for [Practice Name] to a client who hasn't visited in over 18 months. Their pet's name is [pet name]. Don't make them feel guilty. Remind them we're here, mention that [pet name] may be due for a wellness check, and make it easy to book. Keep it warm and under 150 words."

One Last Thing

After practicing with these prompts, I'm confident you'll find plenty of other ways to put AI to work in your practice. Get creative with it. The more you use it, the more natural it becomes — and the more time it frees up for you and your team to focus on what matters most: the animals and people in front of you.

— Cebron

Download a copy of this AI Prompt Library at **cebronwalker.com/free-resources.**

Scan Me!

APPENDIX D

Website & SEO Checklist for Veterinary Practices

Use this checklist to audit and improve your practice's local search visibility and AI discoverability. Work through each section in order — a strong foundation makes every other effort more effective. Grab a pencil and check off each item as you complete it.

Section 1 — Your Online Foundation

Confirm your clinic name is spelled consistently across important online listings — start with Google Business Profile, Facebook, Apple Maps, Bing Places, and Yelp, then check any veterinary-specific directories (AAHA, VetStreet) and local directories (Nextdoor, Chamber of Commerce) that apply to your practice

- Verify your address is identical on Google, Facebook, Yelp, Apple Maps, and all directories/listings noted above.
- Confirm your phone number is the same everywhere — including your website header and footer (you'd be surprised how many businesses get a new number and years later haven't gotten all listings and directories and even their website pages updated!)
- Check that your website URL is correct and consistent across all listings
- Ensure your business hours are accurate on your website and Google Business Profile.

- Search your clinic name and look for any duplicate or outdated listings — remove or correct them
- If you haven't already, claim your listing on Yelp, Apple Maps, Bing Places, and any veterinary-specific directories and update them with pictures and other information
- Confirm your practice is listed on at least one veterinary-specific directory (e.g., AAHA, VetStreet)

Inconsistency in your name, address, or phone number — known as NAP consistency — confuses both Google and AI search tools and lowers your visibility. Search your clinic name plus city on Google and note every listing that appears. Each one is an opportunity to verify or correct.

Section 2 — Your Google Business Profile

- Claim and verify your Google Business Profile if you haven't already
- Confirm business name, address, phone, website, and hours are accurate
- Select the correct primary category (e.g., "Veterinarian") and add relevant secondary categories
- Add all services your clinic offers — be specific (dentistry, spay/neuter, exotic care, cold laser, ultrasound, etc.)
- Upload at least ten photos: team members, exam rooms, lobby, exterior with signage, real patients with permission. If your profile already has many photos, add at least 5 new pictures.
- Add a short, keyword-rich business description that includes your location and key services

- Enable messaging so clients can text you directly from your Google listing
- Set up Google Posts — post at least once per week (tips, seasonal reminders, team highlights)
- Review and respond to every Google review — positive and negative — within 48 hours
- Ensure your booking link is active and working if you offer online scheduling
- Add your clinic's attributes (e.g., "identifies as women-led," "wheelchair accessible," "accepts new patients")

Your Google Business Profile is often the first and only page a new client sees before deciding to call. Treat it with the importance it deserves. Fresh photos uploaded weekly improve your profile's visibility in local search results. Responding to reviews — especially negative ones — demonstrates professionalism and builds trust with prospective clients who are reading those exchanges.

Section 3 — Your Website Service Pages

- Confirm you have a dedicated service page for each major service you offer
- Each service page should include: what the service is, who it's for, what to expect, and a clear "Book Now" call to action
- Use plain, client-friendly language — avoid medical jargon wherever possible
- Include the name of your city or region naturally within service page content

- Add species-specific pages if you treat multiple animal types (dogs, cats, exotics, equine, farm animals)

- Include real photos or video on each service page — no stock imagery

- Add three to five Frequently Asked Questions at the bottom of each service page

- Ensure every service page has a clear headline, a meta description, and a page title that includes the service name

- Link related service pages to each other (e.g., dental cleaning page links to anesthesia safety page)

- Confirm all service pages are mobile-friendly and load quickly on a phone

- Add schema markup (structured data) to your service pages — ask your web developer or marketing provider

Pet owners search for specifics: “rabbit vet near me,” “dog dental cleaning,” “cat vomiting but eating.” If you don’t have a page that addresses those terms, you won’t appear in those searches.

Section 4 — AI Visibility & AI Search Optimization

- Review your homepage and service pages — is every page written in clear, plain, specific language?

- Confirm your clinic’s name, location, and specialty are clearly stated on every major page of your website

- Check that your Google reviews are recent — aim for at least two to four new reviews per month consistently

- Ensure your website has an updated sitemap submitted to Google Search Console

- Confirm your website loads quickly and is fully mobile-responsive

- If you don't have one, add an "About Us" page that clearly describes your clinic's history, team, specialties, and location

- Include your city and region name naturally throughout your website content — not just in the footer

- Ask your web developer or marketing provider whether your site has been optimized for AI discovery — structured signals, discovery hub pages, and AI crawler tracking

- Review your presence on third-party sites that AI tools reference — Yelp, Healthgrades, Facebook, veterinary directories

- Confirm that your practice description is consistent across Google, Yelp, Facebook, and your website

AI tools like ChatGPT and Google Gemini make local recommendations based on the clarity, consistency, and credibility of your digital presence. The stronger your foundation across Sections 1 through 3, the more visible you become to AI search. AI Search Optimization, or ASO, is a behind-the-scenes infrastructure layer that helps AI systems discover, understand, and reference your website with greater confidence. Ask your marketing provider whether your site currently has ASO in place.

Section 5 — Quick Wins You Can Do This Week

- Search your clinic name on Google and note every listing — correct any inconsistencies
- Upload three new photos to your Google Business Profile today
- Add or update your services list inside Google Business Profile
- Respond to any unanswered Google reviews
- Ask your front desk team: "What do callers ask most often?" Get at least 4 things that get asked the most about — use those questions as FAQ material
- Write one new Google Post — called an "Update" — this week (a seasonal tip, a team highlight, or a service reminder)
- Check that your website homepage clearly states who you serve, where you are, and what makes you different
- Ask a team member to search "vet near me" on their phone and see where your practice appears

How Did You Do?

- **40 or more items checked:** Excellent foundation — focus on AI visibility and content freshness
- **25 to 39 items checked:** Strong start — prioritize your Google Business Profile and service pages
- **Under 25 items checked:** Begin with Section 1 and work forward — every improvement compounds over time

---

A printable version of this checklist is available as a free download at **cebronwalker.com/free-resources.**

Scan Me!

APPENDIX E

Your 90-Day Practice Growth Plan

This plan brings together everything in this book into one simple, sequential checklist. It doesn't introduce anything new — it simply tells you what to focus on, in what order, and where to find the tools you need. Work through it one phase at a time. Check items off as you complete it.

There is a lot involved in marketing a veterinary practice. If you have a marketing agency team supporting you, that's great — now, with the knowledge from this book, you and your agency are an even more effective team together. Use this checklist alongside your agency to make sure everything is firing on all cylinders for the best possible outcomes.

Days 1–30: Foundation

Focus: Message clarity, online foundation, and Google Business Profile

- Write your core message using the worksheet in Chapter 3
- Build your ideal client persona using Appendix A
- Run a Digital Footprint Audit — Section 1 of Appendix D
- Confirm your name, address, and phone number are consistent across these key directories:
    - ◊ Google Business Profile
    - ◊ Facebook Business Page

    - ◊ Apple Maps (Apple Business Connect)
    - ◊ Bing Places
    - ◊ Yelp
    - ◊ Nextdoor
    - ◊ Any veterinary-specific directory (AAHA, VetStreet)
    - ◊ Your local Chamber of Commerce directory, if applicable

- Claim, verify, and complete your Google Business Profile — Section 2 of Appendix D
- Upload at least ten new photos to your Google Business Profile
- Review your website homepage — does it clearly state who you serve and what makes you different? (Chapter 3)
- Set your Google review request process in motion using the scripts in Chapter 5
- Introduce your Front Desk Call Handling Playbook to your team — Appendix B
- Hold your first team role-play session using Part 5 of Appendix B

Days 31–60: Visibility and Trust

Focus: Website, content, social media, and reviews

- Complete Section 3 of Appendix D — confirm every major service has its own clear, well-written page
- Add three to five FAQs to your top two service pages
- Begin posting two to three times per week on social media — see content ideas in Chapter 6

- Start your new client welcome sequence — Chapter 9
- Set up your post-visit and post-procedure follow-up calls — Appendix B, Part 4
- Review your last 90 days of Google reviews — are you averaging at least two to four new reviews per month?
- Use the AI Prompt Library — Appendix C — to draft your next round of social posts and Google updates
- Complete Section 4 of Appendix D — AI visibility checklist
- Ask your web developer or marketing provider whether AI Search Optimization (ASO) is in place

---

Days 61–90: Demand and Momentum

Focus: Advertising, conversion, and loyalty systems

There is a lot involved in running effective ad campaigns. If a marketing agency is handling this for you, that's great — this checklist gives you the language and the standards to ask the right questions and make sure everything is being done well.

- Choose one service to promote — Chapter 7's "Exercise for Your Clinic"
- Confirm you have a matching landing page for that service before launching any ad
- Set your budget for the campaign
- Launch your first campaign — Google Search, Meta, or both
- Confirm your speed-to-lead standards are being met — Appendix B, Part 1

- Run your Loyalty Self-Assessment — Chapter 9
- Schedule your first "Experience Your Practice Like a Client" exercise — Chapter 8
- Review your numbers: ad spend, leads, booked appointments, and new clients (Chapter 7, Measurement)
- Identify one thing that's working well and one thing to improve — then repeat the cycle

---

At the End of 90 Days

You won't have built a perfect practice. No one does. But you will have built a system — one that gets stronger the longer it runs. Return to this checklist often, improving everytime.

You can print off a hard copy version of this 90-Day Practice Growth Plan at **cebronwalker.com/free-resources.**

Scan Me!

APPENDIX F

Marketing Glossary for Modern Business Owners

A personal note:

Marketing people love acronyms and jargon. Most of it isn't meant to confuse you on purpose — it's just how the industry talks to itself, the same way you and your team use medical shorthand that would leave a regular pet owner completely lost. But here's the thing: if you don't understand the words your marketing agency is using, it's hard to know if they're doing a great job or just talking over your head.

I wrote this glossary so you'd never feel lost in the conversation again.

— Cebron

Section 1 — Search & Websites

SEO (Search Engine Optimization): Making your website easier for Google to find and show to people searching for things like "vet near me." Think of it as making your storefront sign bigger and clearer so people walking by can find you.

Local SEO: SEO, but specifically for showing up when someone nearby searches for a business like yours. This is the most important kind of SEO for a veterinary practice. For example, making sure your Google Business Profile is fully filled out and kept up to date — accurate hours, current photos, the right categories — is one of the simplest and most powerful things you can do for local SEO. It's often the very first thing a nearby pet owner sees about your practice.

Keyword: A word or phrase someone types into Google. "Vet near me" is a keyword. Your town, such as "Boise" is a keyword. So is "dog won't eat."

Backlink: When another website links to your website. Google sees this like a vote of confidence — the more good websites that link to you, the more trustworthy you look.

Landing Page: The specific page on your website someone lands on after clicking an ad. If your ad is about dental cleanings, the landing page should be about dental cleanings — not your homepage.

Schema Markup (also called "Structured Data"): Invisible labels added to your website's code that help Google and AI tools understand what's on the page — like telling them "this is a phone number" or "this is a list of FAQs." You don't see it, but computers do.

Meta Description: The short summary of a page that sometimes shows up under your website's link in Google search results.

Sitemap: A simple list of every page on your website, given to Google so it can find and understand your whole site easily.

Core Web Vitals: Google's way of measuring how fast and smooth your website feels to use. Slow, clunky websites score poorly and rank lower.

NAP Consistency: Short for **N**ame, **A**ddress, **P**hone number. This means your business information matches exactly everywhere it appears online — Google, Facebook, Yelp, your website. Mismatched information confuses search engines and lowers your visibility.

Section 2 — AI Search Terms (New and Important)

This is genuinely new territory, and the terms are still settling.

Here's what you need to know in plain language:

AI Search: When someone gets an answer from a tool like ChatGPT or Google's AI Overview instead of a list of website links. The AI reads the internet and gives one direct answer.

LLM (Large Language Model): The technology behind tools like ChatGPT, Claude, and Google Gemini. Think of it as a very well-read assistant that has read a huge amount of text and can answer questions in natural, human-sounding language.

AI Overview: Google's own AI-generated summary that sometimes appears at the top of search results, answering your question directly before you even see the list of websites below it.

AEO (Answer Engine Optimization): Making your content easy for AI tools to pull out and use as a direct answer. If someone asks "what's the best vet for exotic pets near me," AEO is about making sure your website is written in a way that gives the AI a clear, ready-made answer to repeat.

GEO (Generative Engine Optimization): Very similar to AEO — making sure AI tools like ChatGPT and Gemini understand your business well enough to mention or recommend you when someone asks a relevant question. Think of GEO as the bigger umbrella term, and AEO as one part of it.

ASO (AI Search Optimization): A general term covering all the technical work done behind the scenes on your website so AI search tools can find, understand, and trust your content. This includes things like clean website code, clear writing, and structured data.

AI Visibility: How often — and how accurately — your business shows up when people ask AI tools questions related to what you do.

Citation (in AI search): When an AI tool actually mentions or recommends your business by name in its answer. This is the AI search version of showing up at the top of Google.

Zero-Click Search: When someone gets their full answer directly from the AI or search engine and never actually clicks through to a website. This is becoming more and more common — which is exactly why being mentioned by name matters so much now, even if it doesn't always send someone to your website.

Hallucination (AI term): When an AI tool confidently states something that simply isn't true. This is why it's important to keep your business information accurate and consistent everywhere online — it reduces the chances of an AI getting your details wrong.

Prompt: The question or instruction someone types into an AI tool. "What's the best vet near me for a sick cat" is a prompt.

Section 3 — Advertising Terms

PPC (Pay-Per-Click): A type of online ad where you only pay when someone actually clicks on it. Google Search Ads work this way.

CPC (Cost Per Click): How much you pay, on average, every time someone clicks your ad.

CTR (Click-Through Rate): The percentage of people who see your ad and actually click on it. A higher number generally means your ad is doing a good job grabbing attention.

Impressions: The number of times your ad was shown to someone — whether they clicked it or not.

Conversion: When someone takes the action you wanted — booking an appointment, calling your office, filling out a form. This is the actual goal of most advertising.

CAC (Cost to Acquire a Client): How much money you spend, on average, in advertising to get one new client.

LTV (Lifetime Value): How much revenue one client is worth to your practice over time — usually measured over their first year or two as a client.

ROAS (Return on Ad Spend): A simple way to measure whether your ads are worth the money. If you spend $1,000 on ads and it brings in $5,000 in business, your ROAS is 5x — meaning you got five dollars back for every one dollar spent.

Retargeting: Showing ads again to people who already visited your website or watched one of your videos but didn't book. It's a gentle reminder that says, "we're still here when you're ready."

Ad Extension: Extra information attached to a Google ad — like your phone number, address, or hours — that makes the ad more useful and trustworthy at a glance.

Boosted Post: Paying a small amount of money to show a regular social media post to more people. This is different from a real ad campaign, which has specific targeting and goals built in.

Section 4 — Social Media & Content Terms

Organic (content or reach): Content that reaches people naturally, without paying for ads. A regular Facebook post that people see because they follow your page is organic.

Engagement: Likes, comments, shares, and reactions on a social media post. High engagement usually means people genuinely found the content interesting or relatable.

Share: When someone takes your content and posts it to their own page or sends it to a friend. This is one of the most valuable metrics in social media — a share means your content was good enough that someone wanted other people to see it too. A handful of shares from real clients is often worth more than hundreds of likes.

UGC (User-Generated Content): Content created by your actual clients — like a photo or video they post themselves about their pet's visit. This is one of the most powerful and trustworthy types of marketing because it comes from real people, not the business itself.

Algorithm: The computer system that decides what content gets shown to which people on platforms like Facebook, Instagram, and Google. Nobody outside the company knows exactly how it works — but it generally rewards content that feels genuine and gets real engagement.

Reach: The number of different people who saw your content.

Impressions vs. Reach: Impressions count every time content was shown — even to the same person multiple times. Reach counts unique people who saw it at least once.

Follower: Someone who has chosen to see your business's posts regularly on a platform like Instagram or Facebook.

Section 5 — Reputation & Trust Terms

Trust Signal: Anything that helps a potential client feel confident choosing your business — reviews, testimonials, photos of real people, awards, and so on.

Social Proof: Evidence that other people have used and liked your business. Reviews, testimonials, and UGC are all forms of social proof.

Reputation Management: The ongoing work of monitoring, responding to, and improving what people say about your business online — mainly through reviews.

Recency Bias: People naturally trust businesses that seem recently active over ones that seem to have gone quiet — even if the quiet business is just as good. This is why posting and getting reviews consistently matters more than doing it once and stopping.

Section 6 — General Business & Marketing Terms

Brand: The overall feeling, reputation, and personality people associate with your business — not just your logo.

Personal Branding: Building a reputation and following around you, specifically — not just your business. Many veterinarians and practice owners benefit from this in addition to their practice's brand. If you become a known, trusted voice in your community — through social media, speaking, writing, or even a book — people trust your practice more because they already trust you. This becomes especially valuable if you ever plan to write a book, launch a course, speak at conferences, or build something beyond your practice's four walls.

Funnel: A simplified way of describing the journey someone takes from first hearing about your business to becoming a client. Picture a funnel shape — wide at the top (lots of people aware of you) and narrow at the bottom (fewer people who actually book).

Flywheel: A growth model where each part of your marketing reinforces the next, building momentum over time — used throughout this book to describe how veterinary practice growth really works.

CRM (Customer Relationship Management): Software used to track and manage relationships with clients — contact information, appointment history, communication, and more. Many practice management systems include CRM features.

KPI (Key Performance Indicator): A specific number you track to measure whether something is working — like new clients per month, or your average Google review rating.

A/B Testing: Trying two different versions of something — like two ad headlines — to see which one performs better.

A printable, updated version of this glossary is available as a free download at **cebronwalker.com/free-resources**, and will be updated periodically as new terms emerge.

Scan Me!

ABOUT THE AUTHOR

Cebron Walker

Cebron Walker is the Founder, CEO, and Chief Creative Officer of Walker Kreative, a USA Today Top 10 Digital Marketing Agency with offices in Clearwater and St. Petersburg, Florida, and Sacramento, California. For more than 35 years, Cebron has helped businesses — from Fortune 500 companies to independent community clinics — build marketing systems that actually work, grounded in clarity, trust, and genuine human connection.

Over the past decade, Cebron has focused much of his work on the veterinary industry, partnering with independent practice owners across the country to help them grow predictable, healthy practices without sacrificing the compassionate, community-first values that brought them into the profession in the first place. Veterinary Marketing: A Handbook for Practice Growth is the culmination of that work — a practical, step-by-step system built specifically for the realities of running a veterinary practice in the AI era.

Cebron's approach is rooted in a simple belief: marketing should never feel like a gimmick or a guessing game. It should be a clear, ethical system that earns trust, attracts the right clients, and gives practice owners their time and energy back — so they can focus on what they love most: caring for animals and the people who love them.

When he's not building marketing systems for veterinary practices, Cebron can be found collecting Silver Age comic books, spending time with his wife Angela and their children Matteo and Natalya, or exploring his next personal project. He lives in Florida and continues to lead Walker Kreative's mission of helping independent practice owners build businesses — and lives — they're proud of.

To connect with Cebron, access free resources from this book, or learn more about working with Walker Kreative, visit **cebronwalker.com.**

Scan Me!

www.ingramcontent.com/pod-product-compliance
Lightning Source LLC
LaVergne TN
LVHW100310210926
848480LV00003B/1081